STAYING HEALTHY

IN ASIA, AFRICA, AND LATIN AMERICA

STAYING HEALTHY

■ IN ASIA, AFRICA, ■
AND LATIN AMERICA

DIRK G. SCHROEDER, Sc D, MPH

A VIA BOOK

STAYING HEALTHY IN ASIA, AFRICA, AND LATIN AMERICA

Please send all comments, corrections, additions, amendments, and critiques to:

Dirk G. Schroeder
℅ Moon Publications
P.O. Box 3040
Chico, CA 95927-3040 USA

Published by
Moon Publications, Inc.
P.O. Box 3040
Chico, CA 95927-3040, USA

Printed by
Griffin Printing

Library of Congress Cataloging-in-Publication Data

Staying Healthy in Asia, Africa, and Latin America / by Dirk G. Schroeder
   p.   cm.
   Originally published: Stanford, Calif. : Volunteers in Asia, 1988.
   Includes bibliographical references and index.
   ISBN 1-56691-011-0 : $10.95
   1. Travel—Health aspects—Developing countries—Handbooks, manuals, etc.
2. Medicine, Rural—Developing countries—Handbooks, manuals, etc. 3. Tropical
medicine—Developing countries—Handbooks, manuals, etc. 4. First-aid in illness and
injury—Developing countries—Handbooks, manuals, etc. I. Title.
RA783.5.S34   1993   92-44954
613.6'8'091724—dc20   CIP

Printed in the United States of America

Contents

Preface

The need for a book of this kind was identified over a decade ago by Volunteers in Asia, Inc. (VIA). As an organization that has sent over 1,000 volunteers to live and work in Asia over the past 30 years, VIA developed a good understanding of the health concerns of foreigners living overseas.

In 1979, the book *Staying Healthy in Asia* was published to provide health information for VIA volunteers as well as other individuals who were living in less-developed areas of Asia.

In 1988, I authored an expanded version of this text entitled *Staying Healthy in Asia, Africa, and Latin America: Your Complete Health Guide to Traveling and Living in Less-Developed Regions of the World*, published by VIA. This book met with such success that VIA and I decided to publish the second edition of this work with Moon Publications; we are excited about the collaboration with Moon and its potential to provide wider access to this information.

During the writing of this and the previous versions of *Staying Healthy in Asia, Africa, and Latin America,* many people have given their time, encouragement, and expertise.

As stated above, this book has built upon the work and ideas of others. Specific recognition goes to David Laney and Anne Huckins, the editors of the first and second editions of *Staying Healthy in Asia,* respectively. The format and tone of the current book have drawn heavily from these earlier publications.

A special thanks to the Hesperian Foundation; to Jane Maxwell for her detailed editorial comments; and to David Werner, author of *Where There Is No Doctor,* who generously allowed us to adapt sections of his book (including illustrations) for our chapters 4, 6, and 8.

The following health professionals read parts of the manuscripts of the first or second editions of the current book: Jan Lahr, Dr. John Dorman, Dr. Paul Basch, Bob Valentine, Anna Marcovich-Kozlowski, Dr. Reynaldo Martorell, Jeff Swisher, Dr. Henry R. Hilgard, Dr. Stephen D. Sears, Dr. John M. King, and Dr. Ruben F. del Prado. I am grateful to all of these people for their comments, although any errors are mine.

Editorial, organizational, and publishing support have been given by: Paul Strasburg, John Morris, Anne Huckins, Mike Saxenian, Greg James, Julia H. Hilgard, and Karie Brown. Thanks to my sister, Kristen Schroeder, who drew several illustrations.

Alissa Keny-Guyer, executive director of VIA, was instrumental in making this update a reality. Thanks also to Joe Cummings for his guidance and recommendations on publications options.

Dwight Clark, founder and president of VIA, deserves unique recognition for his unique vision and his total commitment to cross-cultural living and learning.

On a personal note, I would like to acknowledge my parents, Mary Linda Cook and Dr. John Speer Schroeder, who have provided me with the values that made my contribution to this book possible.

Finally, a very special *gracias* to my wife Carmen, whose patience, support, and assistance made working on this edition a joy.

—Dirk G. Schroeder, Sc D, MPH
Ithaca, New York, November 5, 1992

■ ABOUT THE AUTHOR

Dr. Dirk Schroeder brings over fifteen years of academic and overseas experience to *Staying Healthy in Asia, Africa, and Latin America.* As an undergraduate at Stanford University, Schroeder spent a year in Indonesia with the Volunteers in Asia Program, seeing firsthand the daily realities of the rural poor. Upon graduation, he returned to Indonesia as a Fulbright scholar to research the health and nutrition needs of West Javanese; a bout of typhoid during this time convinced him of the need for a book of this kind.

At Johns Hopkins University for graduate school, Schroeder received a Masters in Public Health and a Doctor of Science from the Department of International Health. Heading south for his doctoral field work, he conducted investigations on child nutrition in a Mayan village in the highlands of Guatemala in conjunction with the Institute of Nutrition for Central America and Panama (INCAP). Currently, Dr. Schroeder continues his work on health issues of developing countries as a Research Associate at Cornell University.

Introduction

■ THE PURPOSE OF THIS BOOK

Becoming sick while living or traveling in a developing country* can turn an exciting adventure into an ordeal. Knowing this, many people heading to Asia, Africa, or Latin America have two questions in mind: 1) "How can I avoid becoming sick?" and 2) "If I do become sick or injured, what steps should I take if medical care is not immediately available?"

This book has been written to provide answers to these questions and to allow you to have a healthy, and thus enjoyable, trip.

■ WHO IS THIS BOOK FOR?

This book is for anyone going to the developing world, from the vacationing tourist to the foreign volunteer living a day's walk from the nearest medical care.

If you are a businessperson or short-term tourist who will stay on well-traveled routes, this manual provides guidelines to immunizations and the basic rules of eating, drinking, and personal hygiene—which, if followed, will help keep you from spending your limited time confined to bed or the bathroom.

This book is also written for students, foreign volunteers, teachers, budget travelers, consultants, and researchers—anyone who will live or travel off the beaten path in the Third World. If you count yourself among these adventurers, this manual provides information on long-term health maintenance, as well as specific instruction in case

---

* In this book, the terms "developing countries," "Third World," "developing world," and "less-developed countries" are used interchangeably. In doing so, I am not making value judgments comparing different parts of the world. Rather, these terms are used only as a matter of convenience to refer to areas of the world that have poor sanitation facilities, few government health and hygiene controls, and a high level of infectious and parasitic diseases.

you are sick or injured and medical help is not available.

The first three chapters are oriented towards **prevention of illness** and include information on immunizations, malaria pills, the basic rules of hygiene, and general health maintenance. Follow the guidelines laid out in these sections closely, especially when you first arrive. Many, if not most, sicknesses suffered by foreign travelers are preventable; do what you can to avoid them.

The majority of the rest of the book describes the **diagnosis and treatment** of common, and not so common, illnesses and first-aid emergencies. Although these sections are to be used when someone is already sick and injured, reviewing this material beforehand will give you additional insight into the prevention of these ailments.

■ CONCLUSION

It is my hope that *Staying Healthy in Asia, Africa, and Latin America* will help you to feel more confident while traveling or living in the less-developed areas of the world. Without negating the health problems that exist in these areas, it is reassuring to realize that the main factors that determine how healthy you are—proper immunization, food and water intake, personal cleanliness, and mental attitude—are things over which you have a great deal of control. I encourage **you** to take good care of yourself, and enjoy.

■ IS THIS BOOK OUT OF DATE?

Every effort has been made to keep abreast of the latest health reporting and regulations, but the situation is changing constantly. Help us keep this book in shape! Please write to let us know about any inaccuracies or new information. Address your letters to:

Dirk G. Schroeder
C/o Moon Publications
P.O. Box 3040
Chico, CA 95927-3040

■ ABBREVIATIONS

AIDS	—	Acquired Immunodeficiency Syndrome
AMS	—	acute mountain sickness
ARC	—	AIDS-related Complex (now called HIV disease)
cc	—	cubic centimeters
CDC	—	Centers for Disease Control
CPR	—	cardiopulmonary resuscitation
HIV	—	Human Immunodeficiency Virus
IG	—	immune globulin
IM	—	intramuscular
IUD	—	intrauterine device
kg	—	kilogram
lbs	—	pounds
mg	—	milligram
NGU	—	nongonococcal urethritis
NGV	—	nongonococcal vaginitis
OPV	—	oral polio vaccine
PABA	—	para-aminobenzoic acid
PID	—	pelvic inflammatory disease
pH	—	acid/alkaline balance
PMS	—	premenstrual syndrome
PPNG	—	penicillinase-producing *Neisseria gonorrhoeae*
RDA	—	Recommended Daily Allowance
STD	—	sexually transmitted disease
WHO	—	World Health Organization

■ IMPORTANT!

Staying Healthy in Asia, Africa, and Latin America is designed to provide general health information and should not be used as a comprehensive medical text.

Although the usual treatments of certain illnesses and emergencies are included in this guide, these are given to help the reader to make more informed decisions and are not intended as a substitute for trained medical help.

All medical and medicinal treatment is best carried out under the direct supervision of a trained physician or health worker. Self-treatment is discouraged and should be undertaken only in emergency situations far from medical care.

The publisher and author disclaim responsibility for any deleterious effects that result from actions taken by an individual using information found in this book.

Before You Go

Getting ready to go to a less-developed region of the world requires preparation. Planning ahead, taking necessary precautions, and gathering supplies prior to your departure will keep you healthier, and thus happier, when you get overseas. The following is a checklist of things that should be done before you go.

PRE-DEPARTURE CHECKLIST

- ☐ **Itinerary (travel plans):** Anticipate which countries you will visit, for how long, and in what order, as well as whether you will be spending extended periods of time in rural areas where diseases tend to be more common. This information is necessary for making decisions on immunizations, malaria pills, health supplies, and clothing.

- ☐ **Medical Check-up:** Be sure you are healthy before you leave by getting a general physical. A dental exam, eye exam, tuberculin skin test, and (for women) a Pap smear are a good idea if you will be gone for a long time. You may also consider getting tested for HIV (which causes AIDS) if you will be away a long time (see pp. 112-115). Check your medical history to see if you have any allergic reactions to certain medications. Get a note from your doctor describing these allergies and be sure to note both common and chemical names. Know and record on a travel document your blood type.

- ☐ **Immunizations (see pp. 3-9):** Getting properly immunized is perhaps the most important preventive health measure you can take as you prepare to go to the developing world.

- ☐ **Malaria Pills (see pp. 9-13):** If you are going to an area where there is malaria, you should start taking malaria pills 1-2 weeks before your arrival.

☐ **Health Supplies (see pp. 15-19):** Included is a list of the health and medical supplies you should consider carrying with you. If you are going to be in a remote area for a long time, bringing more specialized drugs and supplies with you may be appropriate. **Discuss the proper use of these with your doctor.**

☐ **Proper Clothing (see p. 19):** Determine the climatic conditions of your destination at the time of year you are going. Also, be aware of cultural constraints (e.g., shorts and sleeveless shirts are not appropriate in some Muslim societies).

☐ **Contact IAMAT (see p. 20):** IAMAT (International Association for Medical Assistance to Travelers) provides a wealth of services for travelers, including a list of English-speaking doctors overseas.

☐ **Specialized Books (see pp. 174-175):** Although *Staying Healthy in Asia, Africa, and Latin America* is designed to be quite comprehensive, if you will be living or working in extremely remote areas or under unusual circumstances, you may want to take more specialized texts. Refer to the booklist at the back of this book; *Where There Is No Doctor* is recommended.

☐ **First-aid Course:** It is suggested that you take a first-aid course (available through the Red Cross, local clinics, and some schools) before you leave, especially if you will be far from quality medical care. Learn to do cardiopulmonary resuscitation (CPR) which may be offered in a separate or more advanced course. The skills you acquire through these classes will enable you to be better prepared to attend to yourself or others in emergency situations.

☐ **Plan for Medical Emergencies:** Gather information about the area(s) you will be visiting and the medical resources that will be available before you go. The AIDS epidemic (see pp. 112-115) has increased the risk of receiving certain medical procedures (e.g., blood transfusions [see p. 14] and administration of immune globulin [see p. 6]) in less-developed countries, so planning ahead is important.

IMMUNIZATIONS

In the less-developed regions of the world, immunizable diseases are prevalent and you should protect yourself against those to which you may be exposed.

Which vaccinations* you should get is dependent upon your travel plans. Once you have determined your itinerary, consult with your doctor, local clinic, or health department about the current immunization requirements and recommendations. The summary of immunizations outlined on pages 6-9 can be used as a checklist and reference for discussing your individual needs and choices. It is important to **begin the process of getting immunized early** since some series can take weeks or even months.

The most comprehensive information on immunizations is available in the publication *Health Information for International Travelers,* published annually by the Centers for Disease Control (CDC). This booklet includes a description of all available vaccinations as well as a country-by-country listing of vaccination requirements and malaria risk. More up-to-date information is in a biweekly *Summary of Health Information for International Travel* (Blue Sheet), also published by the CDC. Many clinics and specialists have these pamphlets on file or they can be obtained from the U.S. Public Health Service, Division of Quarantine, Centers for Disease Control, Atlanta, GA 30333, or by calling the U.S. Government Printing Office in Washington, D.C. at (202) 783-3238. The CDC also has a 24-hour automated travelers' hotline at (404) 332-4559 that provides information on outbreaks, recommended vaccines by geographic area, clinical management of tropical diseases, HIV and AIDS overseas, and other relevant information.

Private organizations such as IAMAT and Immunization Alert (see pp. 20-21 for addresses) also provide information on worldwide immunization requirements and recommendations for the international traveler.

---

* The terms vaccination and immunization are used synonymously.

■ INTERNATIONAL CERTIFICATE OF VACCINATION

The International Certificate of Vaccination (the "yellow health card") is the document for recording all of your travel immunizations. When you get an immunization, the health specialist that you receive it from will fill out and sign this card. Required vaccinations must be validated by an official stamp (this is usually done at the county health department, but some doctors and clinics have their own official stamp). When you arrive in a country, especially those with strict requirements, customs officials check this card to verify your coverage. If you cannot prove that you have been vaccinated against certain diseases, you may be quarantined or denied entry, or sometimes there is an option of being immunized on the spot (often under less-than-optimal conditions). If you are unable to receive a certain required vaccination for medical reasons, carry a letter from your doctor verifying this and have this letter validated with the official stamp. As with all important documents, it is a good idea to carry photocopies in case of loss or theft.

REQUIRED IMMUNIZATIONS

Currently (November 1992), the only immunization officially **required** for entry into some countries is **yellow fever**. In order to enter countries that require this, you will need to prove, by showing your International Certificate of Vaccination, that you have been properly vaccinated. Vaccination against **cholera** is no longer required for entry into any country, although *local* authorities may continue to request documentation of vaccination.

Some countries are infected with yellow fever, but do not require vaccination for entry. If you have visited one of these countries, you may be required to show proof of vaccination before entering **other** countries—even if the infected country did not require vaccination. Therefore, if you plan to travel from areas classified as endemic (infected) for yellow fever to other countries, you will want to **check the regulations of the countries to which you are traveling**.

The **meningococcal meningitis** vaccine is required for all pilgrims to Mecca, Saudi Arabia.

Note: **Smallpox** has been eradicated throughout the world as of 1980. The smallpox vaccine is no longer required for entry into any country.

COUNTRY-SPECIFIC REQUIREMENTS

Because the vaccination regulations for individual countries change so often, it would be inappropriate to include them in a book of this kind. Consult the CDC or World Health Organization (WHO) publications previously mentioned to determine whether you must receive the yellow fever vaccine, which may be required if you are going to **Africa** (between approximately 15°N and 20°S latitude), **South America** (north of approximately 23°S latitude), or **Panama** (see map, p. 176). Cholera vaccination is no longer officially required by any country, but a few local authorities in Africa ask for documentation of vaccination.

Even if you are not required to get an immunization for entry into a country, it may be advisable to get the yellow fever vaccine anyway if you will be traveling to an area where it is prevalent.

ROUTINE IMMUNIZATIONS

Even in the industrialized world, a number of immunizations are given routinely. You probably got these as a child; however, some require boosters throughout one's lifetime.

As you prepare to go to the Third World, make sure that these **"routine immunizations"** are up to date. If you are going to be staying and eating in "first class," sanitary establishments for a short (less than three week) trip, confirming this coverage and getting the appropriate booster shots may be the only vaccinations you need.

RECOMMENDED IMMUNIZATIONS

Numerous immunizations are neither required nor routine, but are **"recommended"** as protection against some of the diseases commonly found in the developing world. Which of these recommended immunizations you should get will depend on your itinerary and your anticipated living and working situations.

IMMUNIZATIONS FOR CHILDREN, PREGNANT WOMEN, AND BREAST-FEEDING MOTHERS

Some of the immunizations discussed here may not be safe for children or pregnant women. It is important to discuss possible side-effects of vaccines with a doctor or health worker if you are an expectant mother or the parent of a child who will be traveling or living in a developing country. Vaccinations are generally safe for breast-feeding mothers.

IMMUNIZATIONS FOR PEOPLE WITH HIV OR AIDS

HIV-positive individuals, including those with AIDS, should not receive the oral typhoid, oral polio, yellow fever, or plague vaccines. All other vaccines are safe.

BOOSTER SHOTS WHILE IN THE THIRD WORLD

Be careful of the conditions under which immunizations are given. In some countries, it is common to use the same needle for a number of people. This practice substantially increases the risk of contracting hepatitis and AIDS. If conditions look questionable, get the injection somewhere else. You embassy can recommend reliable places to get injections. In many countries you can buy sterile needles and syringes over the counter and take them with you to the doctor's office or clinic. Certain products (e.g., immune globulins) may carry the AIDS virus (HIV) if not properly manufactured. Ask where the vaccine was manufactured and by whom to verify quality.

■ IMMUNIZATION CHECKLIST

ROUTINE AND REQUIRED IMMUNIZATIONS:

(See previous discussion, p. 4.)

These are routine for anyone living in the industrialized world, but you should confirm your coverage and get boosters before you travel.

☐ **Tetanus/Diphtheria**—booster every 10 years.

☐ **Measles/Mumps/Rubella**—(for people born after 1957) one dose of each, good for lifetime if given after 1967.

☐ **Polio**—If fully immunized, get a booster before going overseas.

☐ **Yellow Fever**—single dose, valid for 10 years.

☐ **Cholera**—single dose, valid 6 months. Only 50% effective.

☐ **Meningococcal Meningitis**—single dose, good for 2-3 years.

RECOMMENDED:
If contact with unsanitary conditions is probable:

☐ **Typhoid Vaccine** (see pp. 77-79)— Available either as capsule (oral) or a shot. Orally, 4 capsules (1 every other day) starting 4 weeks before departure. Capsule should be taken with a cool liquid 1 hour before a meal. Repeat series every 5 years. As a shot, 2 shots at least 4 weeks apart, or 3 weekly shots. Booster every 3 years. Vaccine is only 70-90% effective.

☐ **Immune Globulin** (IG, formally referred to as **Gamma Globulin**). Protects against **Hepatitis A** (see p. 92)—single dose, just before departure, booster necessary every **4-6 months**. Overseas, immune globulin is widely available, but make sure it was manufactured in the U.S. (or other industrialized country)—other preparations may not be adequately screened against HIV, the AIDS virus (see pp. 112-115). **Do not** get the shot if you are not sure of its source.

☐ **Tuberculosis Skin Test** (see p. 172)—Take one before departure to establish negative reaction. Repeat test 2-3 months after you return home, or get retested overseas after 1 year.

If traveling to certain areas:
The diseases that these vaccinations protect against occur only in certain areas of the world; consider getting these if you are going to one of these areas.

☐ **Yellow Fever** (see pp. 81-82)—Recommended or required for travel to **Africa** (between approximately 15°N and 20°S latitude), **South America** (north of approximately 23°S latitude), or **Panama**, see map, p. 176.

☐ **Japanese Encephalitis*** (see pp. 83-84)—Recommended for individuals who will spend extended periods (greater than 1 month) in certain rural areas of Asia. Two to three shots, 1-2 weeks apart, booster after 1 year, then every 4 years.

☐ **Meningococcal Meningitis** (see pp. 84-85)—Recommended for long-term travelers to **sub-Saharan Africa** (see map, p. 177), **Tazmania** and **Kenya**, especially during the dry season (December-June). Recent epidemics also reported in **Nepal** and **New Delhi, India**. This vaccine is required for all pilgrims to Mecca, Saudi Arabia.

If working or living under special circumstances:
☐ **Hepatitis B**** (see p. 93)—Recommended for health workers who will be in contact with blood and bodily secretions. It should also be considered by individuals who will be living for extended periods of time in endemic areas (hepatitis B is most prevalent in sub-Saharan Africa and Southeast Asia) or who anticipate sexual contact with the local population in these areas. Two shots at least 4 weeks apart, third dose 5 months after second.

☐ **Cholera** (see pp. 66-67)—Recommended for individuals who will spend long periods of time in areas where there is cholera and who will be living under extremely unsanitary conditions or those who have weakened gastric defense mechanisms (e.g., antacid therapy, ulcer surgery, etc). Vaccine is only 50% effective; a booster is necessary every 6 months.

☐ **Plague** (see pp. 85-86)—Recommended for people who anticipate direct contact with wild rodents or rabbits (e.g., for research) in rural or upland areas. Booster every 6 months.

☐ **Rabies** (see pp. 115-116)—Recommended for specialists (e.g.

---

* The Japanese encephalitis vaccine is presently (November 1992) unavailable in the United States. It is available in Canada, Europe, and countries where Japanese encephalitis is a problem.
** The hepatitis B immunization series takes 6 months to administer and is expensive. The disease can be very serious, however, and we recommend that you protect yourself if there is a chance you will be exposed to it. The vaccine is quite safe and has not been associated

veterinarians, field biologists) as well as children who are frequently exposed to dogs and wildlife in areas where rabies is a threat. Dog rabies is high in Mexico, Guatemala, El Salvador, Columbia, Peru, Ecuador, India, Nepal, Philippines, Sri Lanka, Thailand, and Vietnam and present in many other countries. **Important:** vaccination does *not prevent* rabies; you should still get treatment if you think you were exposed to rabies, even if you got the vaccination.

MALARIA PILLS

A discussion of malaria pills is included here since you should decide on and start an antimalarial drug regimen **before** you arrive in an area where there is malaria (see map, p. 175).

Malaria is transmitted by the bite of an infected mosquito. Malaria parasites invade a person's red blood cells, causing a disease characterized by headache, fever, chills, and sweating. These symptoms subside and then recur over periods of days. Left untreated, the disease may progress to anemia, heart or kidney failure, coma, and even death. (See p. 80 for a more detailed discussion of the life cycle of the malaria parasite and the symptoms of malaria.)

Malaria is best prevented by avoiding mosquito bites (see p. 27). In addition to taking precautions against mosquito bites, you will want to take antimalarial pills if you are going to be in an area where there is malaria. Although malaria pills cannot prevent you from becoming infected, they do inhibit the symptoms of malaria. This called a "suppressive cure."

A variety of factors will determine which malaria pills you should take. First, anticipate where you will be going, for how long, and whether you will be spending extended periods of time in rural areas. Second, determine whether any of the areas you will be going to are re-

---

with causing AIDS. If you do not have time to get all 3 doses of the vaccine, there is still substantial protection after the first 2 doses. If you are not able to obtain the complete series and will be in an endemic areas for longer than 6 months, you may want to carry the third dose with you (refrigerate within 2 weeks of arrival, do not freeze). Find a qualified medical person to administer this final dose using a **sterile** needle (or use the needle that you brought with you). The vaccine is also available in some cities in the Third World.

porting the presence of the *Plasmodium falciparum* (*P. falciparum*) strain of malaria which is resistant to chloroquine (the primary antimalarial drug). If traveling to remote areas, you will need to assess whether medical care will be readily available. Finally, determine whether you have any allergic reaction to a particular antimalarial drug.

■ ANTIMALARIAL DRUG REGIMENS

The following recommendations concerning malaria pills are based on the latest (1992) information published by the CDC. However, the malaria situation changes constantly, as does the understanding of antimalarial drugs, so check with your doctor for any new developments. Also, remember that despite the malaria pills you are taking, it is still possible to get the disease. Know the symptoms of malaria and get medical attention if you ever suffer from these, even after you return home.

For each of the following regimens, **begin taking the antimalarial drugs 1-2 weeks before entering a malarious area.** Starting the antimalarial medication several weeks before you arrive ensures adequate blood levels of the drug and allows you to watch for any early adverse reactions. It also helps to establish a regular pattern for taking the drug (always take it on the same day of the week). Be sure to **continue taking your malaria pills for 6 weeks after the last possible exposure** (see pp. 172-173).

Warning: Be sure to read the section on **side effects of antimalarial drugs** (see p. 12) before you begin a regimen.

REGIMEN A

Any duration of travel or residence in malarious areas that have NOT reported chloroquine-resistant strains of malaria.

☐ **Chloroquine** (Complete name is chloroquine phosphate. Common brand name—*Aralen;* generic brands are cheaper.) Take chloroquine once a week. The recommended adult dose is 500 mg (300 mg chloroquine base).

Caution: Amodiaquine is similar to chloroquine and available overseas but not in the United States. Due to reports of severe adverse reactions to this drug, the CDC ***does not*** recommend amodiaquine as an antimalarial drug.

REGIMEN B

Any duration of travel or residence in areas where chloroquine resistance exists (see map, p. 175).

☐ **Mefloquine.** Adult dose is single 250-mg tablet per week.

Alternatives to mefloquine:

☐ **Doxycycline** alone. For individuals who do not tolerate the alternate mefloquine or chloroquine/*Fansidar* regimens or for travel to the border areas of Thailand, where resistance to the other drugs is widespread. The recommended adult dosage of doxycycline is 100 mg orally once a day.

☐ **Chloroquine** once a week (500-mg tablet) *plus* carry a treatment dose of *Fansidar* (pyrimethamine and sulfadoxine). **Warning: See discussion of side effects, below.**

    This treatment dose of *Fansidar* should be taken as soon as you develop the symptoms of malaria, presumably from a chloroquine-resistant strain, and **only when professional medical care is not immediately available.**

    This self treatment is **only a temporary measure and prompt medical care is essential.** If you take *Fansidar* in this manner, continue to take chloroquine at the same time. The recommended adult treatment dose of *Fansidar* is 3 tablets (75 mg pyrimethamine and 1,500 mg sulfadoxine), orally, all at once.

    In Africa, weekly chloroquine plus **proguanil** (*Paludrine*) (Adult dose: 200 mg *daily*) may be more effective than chloroquine alone. Proguanil is not available in the U.S., but is available in Canada, Europe, and Africa.

■ SIDE EFFECTS OF ANTIMALARIAL DRUGS

☐ **Chloroquine**—rarely causes any serious adverse reactions. It may, however, cause minor side effects such as gastrointestinal disturbances, headache, dizziness, and blurred vision, but these generally do not mean that you should stop taking the drug. Taking the drug after meals may help to reduce the frequency and intensity of these reactions. If you should experience continuing side effects, stop taking chloroquine and ask a doctor for advice on a different antimalarial drug. The common belief that chloroquine causes eye disease is exaggerated: only individuals who take large doses over a long period of time (over 5 years) risk any eye damage.

☐ **Mefloquine**—severe adverse reactions are rare with the prophylactic dose (minor side effects of stomach upset and dizziness usually pass), but more frequent if taken in higher, treatment dosages.

☐ *Fansidar*—has been associated with severe skin reactions. *Fansidar* is dangerous for people who have a history of sulfonamide intolerance. Reactions to *Fansidar* are occasionally serious enough to be fatal. If you take *Fansidar* and suffer from such skin and mucous membrane ailments as itching, redness, rash, mouth or genital sores, or a sore throat—get medical help immediately.

☐ **Doxycycline**—is a tetracycline and has similar side effects, the most common of which is a hypersensitivity to the sun. If you are taking this drug, it is important to protect yourself to prevent a bad sunburn. Also, take doxycycline capsules with a large glass of water and/or with a meal to decrease stomach upset.

☐ **Proguanil**—serious side effects are rare; vomiting, nausea, and hair loss have been reported.

■ ANTIMALARIAL PILLS FOR CHILDREN
AND PREGNANT OR BREAST-FEEDING WOMEN

The U.S. Department of Health recommends that children and pregnant women take **chloroquine** if they are going to be in malarious areas. Chloroquine has *not* been found to have dangerous side effects for these individuals. Older children are generally able to take chloroquine, *Fansidar*, and doxycycline, but in **smaller doses based on age or weight**. Consult a doctor for these dosages. **Caution:** Children weighing less than 30 lbs (15 kg) should not take mefloquine. Children under 8 years old should not take doxycycline. Infants under 2 months should not use *Fansidar*. Overdose with antimalarials may be fatal—keep out of reach of children.

If pregnant or breast-feeding women must go to areas where there is the chloroquine-resistant *P. falciparum* strain of malaria, they should consult with a medical specialist since there are risks associated with antimalarial drugs (mefloquine, *Fansidar*, and doxycycline) other than chloroquine. Mefloquine, *Fansidar*, and doxycycline are NOT recommended for pregnant women.

BLOOD TRANSFUSION
EMERGENCIES

In many developing countries, blood is not adequately screened for the Human Immunodeficiency Virus (HIV) that causes AIDS. In case of an accident or emergency, international travelers may be at risk of contracting HIV through blood transfusions. Though the likelihood of the need for a blood transfusion overseas is very low for most travelers, it is wise for those who will be living in country for extended periods of time to anticipate this need in advance.

Because this is a relatively new problem, the solutions to it are not straightforward. The current WHO principals and guidelines are as follows:

1. Unexpected, emergency blood transfusion is rarely required; there is a tendency for medical personnel to perform *unnecessary* blood transfusions in many areas.

2. Alternatives to blood, including colloid and crystalloid *plasma expanders,* are strongly recommended.

3. Emergency evacuation from areas with questionable supplies is highly recommended if necessary and possible.

The option of donating one's own blood for storage is not recommended for most travelers, but should be considered for long-term residents in areas where the blood supply is known to be infected. For large groups of travelers who are traveling together, an agreement to make blood type and HIV status known so that donations within the group could occur in the case of emergency may be an option.

WHAT TO BRING

■ HEALTH SUPPLIES

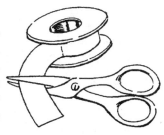

This list provides guidelines for supplies you may want to take with you to the developing world. Although some of these items are available overseas, they may be expensive or difficult to locate. Also, illness tends to strike when you least expect it, so it is best to be prepared and have these items on hand. What you bring will depend on the countries you plan to visit, the length of your stay, and the time of year you go. If you'll be in large cities most of the time, you will need fewer items than if you expect to live or travel in rural areas where medical supplies are harder to find.

All medicines should be clearly labeled, carefully sealed (to prevent spillage and to minimize the effects of humidity), and stored out of direct sunlight. Many medicines and supplies are available under brand names (shown in *italics*) and generic names. Generic drugs tend to be much less expensive, yet equally effective.

Note: A triangle (Δ) indicates an article recommended for individuals who will be in remote areas, far from medical care, for long periods of time.

GENERAL

☐ **Thermometer** in a hard case.

☐ **Toothbrush.** It may be difficult to find "soft" toothbrushes in some countries.

☐ **Dental floss.**

☐ **Tweezers.**

☐ **Scissors.**

□ **Water purification materials.** Iodine tablets (*Potable-Aqua*) are one option (see p. 23).

□ **Extra pair of glasses or contact lenses.** If you wear contacts, bring a supply of lens solutions, since in some countries they are very expensive or unavailable (especially for soft lenses). Many long-term travelers find contact lenses are too difficult to keep clean, so switch to glasses. Bring a copy of your lens prescription.

□ **Contraceptives.** Contraceptives, especially spermicidal jellies and creams, may be difficult to find. Bring an adequate supply of whichever birth control method you use, or if you are going for a long time, arrange to have additional supplies sent to you.

□ **For women: Tampons** are expensive or hard to find in many areas. **Sanitary napkins** are more widely available.

OINTMENTS, CREAMS, AND POWDERS

□ **Sunscreen cream or lotion** (those containing para-aminobenzoic acid (PABA) or oxybenzone are most effective). **Sunblock** (containing zinc oxide or titanium dioxide) is best for extensive or intensive sun exposure. Sunscreen products can be expensive overseas (see p. 52).

□ **Insect repellent.** Repellents with N,N diethylmetatoluamide (DEET) are best (see p. 27).

□ **Calamine lotion** for insect bites.

□ **Baby powder** or **medicated powder** for heat rashes and to prevent fungal infections.

△ **Antibiotic eye ointment** such as polymyxin B-bacitracin (*Polysporin*) for eye infections (make sure the label says "ophthalmic"— for eyes). Eye ointment may be used for treating skin infections, providing that the applicator doesn't get contaminated by touching skin; but never put any ointment in your eyes that is not labeled ophthalmic.

△ **Topical antibiotic cream** (*Neosporin*) for skin infections caused by bacteria.

△ **Anti-fungal powder or cream** such as tolnaftate (*Tinactin*), haloprogin (*Halotex*), clotrimazole (*Lotrimin*), or miconazole (*Micatin*) for fungus infections (see pp. 72-73).

FOR WOUNDS AND INJURIES

☐ **Disinfectant soap** (like *Dial, Betadine*). Thorough cleansing with soap and clean water is the best treatment for cuts and scrapes.

☐ **Adhesive bandages** (*Band-Aids*) to protect small wounds from dirt; moleskin for blisters.

△ **Sterile gauze pads** to control bleeding and to protect burns and large wounds.

△ **Gauze roller bandage**, (2") to hold gauze pads, to control bleeding (to provide direct pressure, rather than to act as a tourniquet), and to hold dressings on hard-to-bandage areas.

△ **Adhesive tape** to hold dressings, close small cuts, help make splints, etc.

△ **Elastic bandage** (*Ace*, 3") to hold gauze pads, to control bleeding (not to act as a tourniquet), and to immobilize sprains and broken bones. Also for use in case of snakebite (see p. 168).

△ *Sawyer Extractor* for removing venom from snakes, scorpions, bees, and spiders *without* cutting the skin (see p. 168).

MEDICATIONS THAT ALL TRAVELERS SHOULD CARRY

☐ **Malaria pills** (for those going to malarious areas, see pp. 9-13, map, p. 175). You will need a prescription from your doctor to get these in the U.S.; they are sold over the counter in many countries overseas.

☐ **Aspirin** or acetaminophen or paracetamol (*Tylenol* or *Datril*) for pain.

☐ **Bismuth-subsalicylate** (*Pepto-Bismol*) for mild diarrhea. Tablets are most convenient. Bring a large quantity since they are difficult to find overseas. Other antidiarrheal medications are discussed on p. 62.

☐ **Promethazine** (*Phenergan*), dimenhydrinate (*Dramamine*), or scopolamine (*Transderm Scop*), for motion sickness.

☐ **Pseudoephedrine** (*Sudafed*) or pseudoephedrine plus triprolidine (*Actifed*) for decongestion accompanying a common cold. Also useful in preventing sinus compression during plane flights.

☐ **Personal medications**. If you take a specialized medicine regularly, carry an adequate, well-labeled supply. A doctor's letter explaining the need for the medication is advisable.

MEDICATIONS AND SUPPLIES TO CONSIDER BRINGING IF MEDICAL CARE WILL NOT BE READILY AVAILABLE

If you are going to be in less-developed areas for a long time and will be far from medical care, you should consider bringing some of the following medications. Consult with your doctor to be certain of correct dosage, usage, and possible side effects. Some medicines require a doctor's prescription.

△ **Antibiotics for infections**. Talk with your doctor. You may want to bring tetracycline, doxycycline, trimethoprim sulfamethoxazole (*Bactrim, Septra*) or another antibiotic. Know how to use these medications (see pp. 43-45).

△ **Metronidazole** (*Flagyl*) for trichomoniasis, amoebic dysentery, etc.

△ Daily **vitamin-mineral supplement** with iron (see pp. 31-32). Does not need to contain amounts greater than 100% Recommended Daily Allowance (RDA).

△ **Codeine** or similar painkiller stronger than aspirin in case of a severe sprain or injury.

△ **Sterile needle** for immunization boosters.

△ *Oralyte* pre-mixed oral rehydration sugar-salt packets for dehydration. You can also make your own formula; follow directions on p. 50.

△ **Acetazolamide** (*Diamox*) for acute mountain sickness (see p. 136).

△ **Nystatin vaginal tablets** (*Mycostatin*) for chronic yeast infection.

■ CLOTHES

In tropical climates, your clothes should be, above all, comfortable. Wear clothing which is loose-fitting and light-colored (but not white, which gets dirty immediately!). Cotton fabric is coolest and most absorbent. Wear comfortable, broken-in shoes or sandals; if you wear socks, use absorbent ones and change them daily. Protect your face and eyes from the sun with dark glasses, a hat, and sunscreen lotion. Be aware that in some cultures it is inappropriate to wear shorts and sleeveless shirts in public (especially if you are a female).

In cold climates, you will want to wear layers of loose-fitting clothing, rather than one heavy jacket. Layering clothes traps your body's warmth and enables you to adjust to different temperatures (especially when hiking). In some countries, indoor heating is rare, so you may be wearing jackets and sweaters indoors. Since up to half of your body heat is lost through your head and hands, a knit hat and mittens can make a great difference in keeping you warm. Wool is still one of the best materials for cold weather because it is economical and continues to insulate even if wet. Down feathers and some synthetic materials (e.g., polypropylene) are also effective, but are more expensive.

ORGANIZATIONS THAT HELP TRAVELERS

There are a number of organizations and clinics that are specifically oriented toward helping international travelers. Travel clinics can be excellent sources of information on immunizations, malaria prevention and other health concerns. These are usually listed in the phone book and may be associated with local universities. Some of the national organizations that help travelers are described below.

■ INTERNATIONAL ASSOCIATION FOR MEDICAL ASSISTANCE TO TRAVELERS (IAMAT)

IAMAT provides a variety of resources for the international traveler. The association has charts of worldwide malaria and schistosomiasis risk, climatic conditions, and immunization requirements. It has also established a worldwide network of English-speaking doctors. IAMAT members receive a city-by-city directory of professionally qualified doctors who speak English or another language in addition to their native language. These doctors have agreed to treat IAMAT members according to a consistent fee schedule: office visit—US$45, house or hotel call—US$55, and night calls, Sundays, and local holidays—US$65.

To become a IAMAT member, write to: IAMAT, 417 Center Street, Lewiston, NY 14092 or call (716) 754-4883. There is no membership fee, but donations are encouraged.

■ IMMUNIZATION ALERT

This computerized service provides up-to-date health and travel information on over 200 countries and territories worldwide. Immunization recommendations and requirements, malaria information, and travel advisories are some of the topics covered in a country-by-country format. Health departments, doctors, and businesses that subscribe to this service receive updated computer diskettes weekly. Information is accessed directly from WHO and is very up-to-date.

If your local health department does not subscribe, individuals can request computer printouts of specific country recommendations by contacting Immunization Alert. Information on one country is US$10, each additional country is US$5. Contact: Immunization Alert, 93 Timber Dr., Storrs, CT 06268; phone: (800) 584-1999; fax: (203) 487-0611.

■ MEDIC ALERT

If you have a serious medical problem (e.g., allergies or diabetes), Medic Alert provides engraved bracelets or necklaces (US$35-65) that identify these ailments in case of emergency. Also on the bracelet is Medic Alert's phone number, to be called collect in the event of an accident or emergency. Additional information (e.g., personal doctor, next of kin) is then accessed. The service is international and interpreters are available. Contact: P.O. Box 1009, Turlock, CA 95381 or call (209) 668-3333.

Arrival And Preventing Illness

Many of the health problems experienced by foreigners living or traveling in the developing world can be avoided by eating well, getting enough rest, and taking a few precautions. In the industrialized world, we are used to being sheltered by established systems of water treatment, sanitation, food inspection, and so on. In most of the Third World, these things cannot be taken for granted; you have to take protective steps yourself. This isn't really difficult—it's just a matter of developing a new awareness about health and hygiene.

Included in this chapter is a discussion of acclimating to your new environment, the basic rules of hygiene, and preventing insect bites. By diligently following the guidelines in this chapter, you will protect yourself against many potential problems. Though it may seem that you are "missing out" by avoiding some foods and taking certain precautions, you will miss out on a lot more if you get sick.

ACCLIMATING

Take it easy the first few days after your arrival. Give yourself a chance to get over jet lag. If you're in a tropical area, the climate will take some adjusting to—drink increased amounts of fluids, go easy on rich, fatty, highly spiced foods and fruits (these can cause diarrhea), and avoid long periods of exposure to the sun. If you are in the mountains, take time to acclimatize; do not gain altitude too quickly (see p. 135).

BASIC RULES OF HYGIENE

Many health problems in developing countries are caused by fecal contamination of water, food, and soil. Diarrheas, dysenteries, some intestinal worms, typhoid, hepatitis A, and cholera are all spread by the fecal-oral (feces to mouth) route.

Avoiding these illnesses depends on three main variables: what you drink, what you eat, and personal cleanliness.

■ WHAT YOU DRINK

WATER

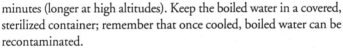

Assume that water is unsafe to drink unless you know otherwise.

The safest and simplest method of water purification is **boiling** for 5 minutes (longer at high altitudes). Keep the boiled water in a covered, sterilized container; remember that once cooled, boiled water can be recontaminated.

When boiling is impractical, you can use a chemical purifier. Iodine is the most effective (**caution:** people with thyroid problems should not use this method without consulting their doctor). Iodine can be used in three different forms: iodine tablets, liquid tincture of iodine (2%) or iodine crystals. Tablets (brand names *Globaline* or *Potable-Aqua*) are less messy than liquid, but the bottle must be kept tightly capped, as dampness or exposure to air drastically reduces the tablets' effectiveness. With tablets, follow the preparation instructions; double for cloudy water. For tincture of iodine, use 2 drops per liter or quart of clear water. After using the tablets or liquid, **allow the water to stand 30 minutes before drinking—longer if water was cloudy**.

To use iodine crystals, you need a 1 oz. (30 cc) clear glass bottle with a leakproof cap, containing 4-8 grams of USP grade resublimed iodine. Fill the bottle with water, shake it vigorously for 30-60 seconds, and hold it upright for a few moments so that the iodine crystals fall to the bottom (the crystals are not to be consumed). Then add $12^1/2$ cc (about half the bottle—you can use the cap to measure) of the water-iodine solution to one liter of water. After standing for 30 minutes, the water should be disinfected. If the water is quite cold or cloudy, allow it to stand at least 40 minutes before drinking—the longer, the better. Only a small amount of the crystal iodine is dissolved each time the bottle is filled with water; the same crystals can be used almost 1,000 times. Keep the bottle filled with water even when not in use—otherwise the iodine vapor will penetrate the cap and damage clothing and metal items.

Caution: Too much iodine is poisonous. Using iodine for water purification is fine on an occasional basis, but it's not safe for continuous use. If you can't boil water, try to drink other liquids—tea, coffee, carbonated drinks—rather than only water that has been iodine-purified.

Chlorine tablets or liquid (laundry bleach) can also be used as a water purifier, but chlorine in drinkable concentrations does not kill amoebas or Giardia, two microorganisms that cause diarrhea and dysentery.

Portable **water filters**, though convenient, are generally unproven in their ability to adequately purify water. The biggest problem is that micropore filters allow viruses to pass and therefore do not protect against hepatitis A, diarrhea-causing viruses, and other diseases. Iodine chemical elements (attachments) are sometimes available and do quite well at overcoming this flaw. (Charcoal- or chlorine-based elements are ineffective.) Because of their lack of proven effectiveness, the CDC does not make a recommendation on filters.

Remember that ice is no safer than the water it was made from. If local water is unsafe, ice will be too unless the water was boiled first. Adding alcoholic beverages does not purify the ice.

Remember to brush your teeth with boiled or chemically purified water, or tea.

OTHER BEVERAGES

When you're eating out, the simplest approach is to avoid water altogether. Stick to coffee or tea, which have been made with boiling water. Beer and wine are usually safe (wipe off the mouth of the bottle or can before drinking). Bottled carbonated drinks usually are safe if they are "name brands," but beware of drinks that could have been bottled in someone's backyard!

Unbottled cold drinks and fresh fruit juices are potentially unsafe, since they are often made with contaminated water, fruit, or milk products—use your judgment.

■ WHAT YOU EAT

You can become sick if you eat food that is contaminated or spoiled. You should be particularly attentive to what and where you eat for the first days and weeks after you arrive. Your intestinal tract will need time to adjust to new bacteria. Over time, your body will adapt and you will be able to more adventurous with the foods you eat without getting sick.

BE PARTICULARLY CAUTIOUS OF THE FOLLOWING:

☐ Raw vegetables and fruits that have been peeled already. Vegetables are often grown with human fertilizer, which may be contaminated. It is nearly impossible to disinfect vegetables simply by washing them, thus vegetables like lettuce are particularly dangerous. When you buy fruits and vegetables, make sure that the skin is unbroken, and peel them yourself. Wash your hands in purified water before you handle food (cooked and boiled vegetables should be safe).

☐ Milk and milk products that may not have been properly pasteurized and kept refrigerated, in which case they offer an excellent breeding ground for bacteria. To be safe, milk should be boiled or used only in foods that will be cooked. Packaged ice cream is usually safe in the big cities; do not buy homemade ice cream off the street. Freshly opened canned milk or powdered milk mixed with purified water is okay.

☐ Pies, custards, gelatins, meringues, and pastries with creamy fillings all require continuous refrigeration to be safe. Don't eat them if in doubt (dry baked goods like bread and cake should be safe).

☐ Meat, poultry, egg dishes, fish, and shellfish should be **thoroughly cooked** and eaten while still hot. Bacteria grow rapidly at room temperature on moist, cooked foods; they can become unsafe within a few hours. Raw clams, oysters, and other shellfish are a common source of hepatitis, while raw meat or fish often contain worms—avoid them (unless you know they are safe).

☐ Flies are active carriers of infection. Try not to eat food on which flies have landed.

☐ Be discriminating about restaurants and street vendors. Although one of the most exciting aspects of being in a foreign culture is trying indigenous foods and dishes, roadside food stalls are notorious for their lack of sanitation and as conduits of disease. If you do choose to eat from these, always check for cleanliness of the food, the utensils, and the vendors who handle the food.

PERSONAL CLEANLINESS

Keep yourself and your clothes as clean and dry as possible. Bathe at least once a day, and dry yourself well, especially between folds of skin where dampness can cause rashes or fungus infections. Using powder may help. Keep your hands and fingernails clean. Avoid biting your nails or licking your fingers. Be sure to wash your hands before handling food or eating.

In a number of countries, the left hand and water are used to wash oneself after defecating (rather than using toilet paper). Be sure to wipe away from your genitals. Obviously, thorough hand-washing is important afterwards.

Always wear shoes or sandals as protection against hookworm and fungus infections. Be careful about sitting on the ground for the same reason. Be careful where you swim or wade. In some areas, rivers or other bodies of fresh water (like flooded rice fields) can harbor snails which carry worms that cause schistosomiasis (see pp. 116-117). Water can also be contaminated with leptospirosis (see p. 87).

PREVENTING INSECT BITES

Many diseases are transmitted by the bite of insects. Mosquitoes transmit such diseases as malaria, yellow fever, filariasis, and encephalitis. Other diseases are passed through the bites of sandflies, ticks, tsetse flies, and fleas. The best protection against these diseases is to **minimize insect bites**. Be familiar with the diseases endemic to your area and the feeding patterns of the insects which carry them. For example, malaria-infested mosquitoes are most likely to bite at dusk and after dark. Cover yourself with long pants and a long-sleeved shirt, and use heavy-weight clothing (mosquitoes can bite through thin cloth) if possible. Spraying permethrin (*Permanone*) on clothing will increase protection. Apply insect repellent to exposed skin.

The most effective ingredient in commercially available repellents is N,N diethylmetatoluamide or DEET. When you buy your insect repellent, get one that contains a high concentration of DEET. The DEET in repellents ranges from 35% to 95% and the higher the percentage, the longer-lasting the protection. **Note:** Some people are allergic to the highest concentrations of DEET. If you use a powerful repellent and have a skin reaction or feel nauseous, try a repellent with a lower concentration of DEET.

Indoors, you might also want to use an insect spray containing pyrethrum to kill insects where they tend to congregate (under beds, in clothes closets, and in dark corners). It is also a good idea to air out your mattress in the sun every few weeks to check for and kill insects that may be hiding there. Finally, protect yourself as you sleep by sleeping inside screened areas or under mosquito netting, by burning mosquito coils, or by running a fan.

General Health Maintenance

For individuals living or traveling in the developing world for an extended period of time, attending to the basics of general health maintenance is important in preventing illness and preserving overall well-being.

Eating a balanced diet, attending to dental hygiene, getting enough exercise, and preserving mental stability are all crucial elements in sustaining a healthy body. Additionally, a fit, well-nourished body can better ward off and recover from illness.

NUTRITION

If you are living or traveling in the developing world and consuming a local diet, you may be concerned that you are not maintaining adequate nutrition. In addition to being unfamiliar with the nutritive value of the foods you are eating, the predominance of carbohydrates and relative lack of meat products can be disquieting.

The best way to make sure that you are eating a nutritious diet is to follow the guidelines outlined below. Eating a variety of foods from each of the different food groups will ensure that you are meeting your body's needs and help you to avoid deficiencies.

■ DAILY NUTRITION GUIDE

Eating foods from the basic food groups outlined here will provide you with a balanced and nutritious diet.

FOOD GROUPS
☐ **Carbohydrate Source Group**
Rice, corn, other grains, bread (whole grain, fortified, or enriched

is best), starchy root vegetables (e.g., potatoes, cassava)
4 or more servings per day

☐ **Protein Source Group**
Meat, poultry, fish, seafood, eggs, soybeans and their products,
dried beans, nuts, and seeds
2 or more servings per day

☐ **Vegetable/Fruit Group**
Dark green, leafy, deep yellow or orange vegetables for vitamin A;
citrus fruits or other high ascorbic-acid foods for vitamin C
4 or more servings per day

☐ **Milk And Dairy Group**
Milk, cheese, yogurt, ice cream. (If no milk products are available,
substitute other protein-and-calcium-rich foods; e.g., soy products, fish, meat, eggs, and some dark green leafy vegetables.)
2 or more servings per day*

Also: Include plenty (8 or more cups) of liquids daily.

■ **THE CONCERN OVER PROTEIN**

In the recent past, it was thought that inadequate protein intake was
central to the problem of malnutrition in the Third World. Today however, research indicates that, for adults, the concern with raising protein levels in traditional diets has been inappropriate. In general, as long
as an adult eats a **varied** diet that contains even small amounts of
animal products such as meat, milk, or eggs, there is little chance of
protein deficiency.

On the other hand, a person consuming a purely vegetarian diet
that contains no animal products will need to be attentive to "complementing" proteins in order to get enough (see following discussion).
Children, since they are growing, will also have more demanding
protein requirements.

---

* Children: 3 or more servings. Teenagers, pregnant or nursing women: 4 or more
  servings.

■ PROTEIN SOURCES AND COMPLEMENTARITY

As stated above, most varied diets will meet protein requirements. Protein needs can be met with foods of both animal and plant origin. In general, proteins from foods of animal origin—meat, fish, eggs, milk, and cheese—are used most efficiently by the body. Plant proteins—grains, legumes, (beans, lentils, and peas), vegetables, seeds, and nuts—tend to be deficient in certain amino acids (the building blocks of proteins) and therefore are not as efficiently used by the body if eaten alone. However, in a meatless or near-meatless diet, you *can* obtain sufficient dietary protein by eating a variety of plant protein foods that "complement" each other.

Protein complementarity is achieved by eating 2 (or more) different types of protein foods in which the amino acids contained in one item are used to supplement the amino acid deficiencies in the other. Since the body is unable to store amino acids, it is necessary to eat these foods within a few hours of each other, most conveniently at the same meal.

The following model* shows the basic non-meat food combinations for maximizing proteins:

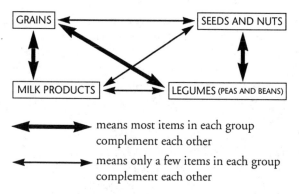

Complementing foods according to this model will allow you to get the most benefit from non-meat sources.

*Model adapted from a chart cited in Francis Moore Lappe's *Diet for a Small Planet* (Ballantine, 1983)

In developing countries, many traditional diets have evolved so that they naturally incorporate foods that complement each other's proteins. For example, in Latin America, rice, beans, and corn balance each other's amino acid strengths and weaknesses. As long as you eat enough of these foods to meet your energy needs, this combination of foods provides enough dietary amino acids for the body to function properly. Similarly in Asia, noodle, soybean products, and vegetables complement each other.

■ PROTEIN AND ENERGY REQUIREMENTS

Protein and energy needs vary from person to person. Factors such as age, weight, sex, and for women, pregnancy and lactation, influence individual requirements. These variables make it difficult to be specific about individual requirements in a book of this kind.

The best way to determine whether your protein and energy needs are being met is to develop an awareness of how you feel—your energy level and temperament—and of your body's overall condition. Weight loss, lethargy, and insomnia may indicate inadequate energy (caloric) intake—consume more foods high in carbohydrates and fats. A sign of protein deficiency is the slow healing of cuts and abrasions. Skin, nails, and hair are also useful protein indicators since they require newly synthesized protein for growth and health.

■ VITAMIN AND MINERAL SUPPLEMENTS

Low-budget travelers or residents in less-developed countries consuming local diets will probably be eating less meat, fewer milk products, and less variety than they normally would at home. Also, foods are less likely to be enriched or fortified and more likely to be cooked or boiled for a long time (which results in vitamin losses). For these reasons, there is a chance that people living on such diets for an extended period of time may become deficient in certain nutrients, vitamins, and minerals. Generally, diets in the Third World are most likely to be deficient in iron (see "anemia," p. 32), calcium, vitamin

B_{12}, vitamin A, and perhaps vitamin D.

A daily vitamin/mineral supplement should be considered by people who feel that their diet may be insufficient to meet their needs. This supplement need not contain amounts greater than 100% of the Recommended Dietary Allowances (RDA)—"mega" doses are unnecessary.

■ EFFECTS OF INFECTION AND ILLNESS ON NUTRITIONAL STATUS

Infection and illness cause decreased absorption of dietary nutrients as well as loss of appetite. In sickness or recovery, this combination can result in a state of malnourishment during a time when your body's needs are the greatest. Also, the use of antibiotics can destroy intestinal bacteria that normally synthesize important vitamins. Therefore, it is important that you consume enough calories, protein, vitamins (especially vitamin C) and minerals during sickness and recovery so your body can rebuild damaged tissues.

Some illnesses require special diets during recovery. For example, you should not drink alcohol for a long time after having hepatitis A. Consult a doctor or nutritionist concerning proper diet following a sickness.

■ IRON-DEFICIENCY ANEMIA

Iron-deficiency anemia is very common (usually in women), even in populations eating otherwise nutritionally balanced diets. Individuals eating predominantly carbohydrate diets with few animal proteins or green vegetables are likely to be iron deficient.

Iron is essential for the production of hemoglobin, which is needed to transport oxygen in the blood. Thus, people who suffer from iron-deficiency anemia cannot supply enough oxygen to their tissues.

The symptoms of iron-deficiency anemia include fatigue, weakness, headache, pallor (pale skin), and shortness of breath. This is particularly a problem for women in their reproductive years due to the loss of blood through menstruation and pregnancy. Iron deficiency is also exacerbated by parasitic infections of the intestines which can result in blood loss.

Dietary iron is found in meat (especially organ meats such as liver), animal products (milk and eggs), and some vegetables (such as spinach). However, the type of iron found in vegetables is not absorbed as well as that in meat. Overall iron absorption can be enhanced by eating small amounts of meat and vitamin C-rich foods along with iron-rich vegetable foods.

An iron supplement in the form of ferrous sulfate should be considered.

DENTAL HYGIENE

A complete dental exam is highly recommended before you leave home. Obtaining quality dental care in the less-developed world can be difficult, so be particularly attentive to dental hygiene during your stay.

Brush your teeth several times a day, especially after eating sticky foods and sweets and before bed. Use a soft toothbrush and fluoride toothpaste. Because hectic travel schedules can disrupt your brushing routine, keep your toothbrush readily available. Chewing crisp fruits and vegetables will also help to clean and refresh your mouth during travel.

Caution: Many travelers forget that, in many countries, tap water is not safe, even in the small amount needed to brush your teeth. **Use bottled or boiled water.**

In addition to brushing, use dental floss to clean between teeth and stimulate your gums. Dental floss may be hard to find overseas, so bring some from home.

If your teeth or gums are painful, you may need medical attention. Dental problems, especially cavities, should be dealt with immediately to avoid further decay. If you require dental care while overseas, be certain that the dentist is skilled and reputable. For a list of resources that may be able to help you locate a good dentist, see pp. 46-47.

EXERCISE

Physical activity is necessary for good health. Regular aerobic exercise aids in proper digestion, weight control, muscle tone, cardiopulmonary (heart and lung) maintenance, better sleep, increased stamina, a greater sense of well-being, and even emotional stability. The physical and psychological benefits of exercise are as important while traveling or living in a foreign country as they are at home, so try to establish an exercise routine while overseas. There are two major categories of exercise:

☐ **Aerobic** (with oxygen) exercise is sustained exercise that requires both the use of large muscles and a constant supply of oxygen. Aerobic exercises include brisk walking, jogging, swimming, cycling, fast dancing, and jumping rope.

☐ **Anaerobic** (without oxygen) activities require short, sudden bursts of energy like sprinting or weight lifting. These are not effective in increasing your cardiovascular system, though they do have other benefits (e.g., maintaining muscle tone).

You should try to do some form of aerobic exercise 3 (or more) times a week for at least 20 minutes. Moderate, daily exercise is far better than doing something strenuous once or twice a week. Make sure to begin a workout with 8-10 minutes of stretching, followed by some easy aerobic work for 2-5 minutes. At this point, increase the speed and intensity of the activity. Following the vigorous portion of your workout, it is essential that you cool down. For example, if you have been running, slow down to a brisk walk for 3-5 minutes and then stretch again for 5-10 minutes. Cooling down and stretching will help you avoid injury. Pay attention to your body; if you feel pain, excessive fatigue, faintness, or nausea, it is warning you to stop.

It may be more difficult to get proper exercise in foreign countries than at home due to such factors as climate, cultural norms, lack of privacy, or traffic congestion. So, you will have to be creative in order to keep your body fit.

If open space or privacy is a problem, some activities that can be done at home or in your room include calisthenics (sit-ups and push-ups), stretching, and yoga. Aerobic exercises that can be done in a small space include skipping rope, running in place, and fast dancing.

Outside, brisk walking is still one of the best forms of exercise. Take time to walk to the train station instead of taking a bus or take the "long way" to your destination. Brisk walking will benefit your heart, lungs, and legs—and who knows what wonders you may discover along the way. Swimming is great exercise, if it is available, but be sure the pool is properly chlorinated.

For individuals living overseas, try to join in the sports activities played in the local community. Participating in community volleyball, badminton, or soccer games can be a great way to keep in shape and meet people at the same time. Studying a local form of self-defense or a native dance will give you cultural insight while you exercise.

■ EXERCISING IN THE HEAT

Exercise creates heat which is normally lost through your skin by sweating and evaporation. However, if you exercise in a hot, humid environment, your body may not be able to cool itself, even with heavy sweating. Under these conditions, **dehydration** (see pp. 49-50) and other **heat disorders** (see p. 57) are potential problems. So, if you are going to be exercising in the heat, make sure you follow these guidelines:

☐ Maintain your body fluids with cool water. The first tenet of prevention is adequate hydration before exercise. This is best done by consuming a cup of water 10-20 minutes before a workout, and then, for the duration of the exercise session, take breaks to consume additional water.

☐ When possible, splash yourself with water, which will evaporate and cool your body.

☐ Outside, wear loose-fitting, light-colored cotton clothing and a light-colored hat. Covering the head guards against the sun's radiant energy and will protect you from dehydration.

☐ Exercise during the coolest times of the day and/or in the shade.

■ EXERCISING IN THE COLD

Heavy exercise in cold conditions can result in problems such as frostbite and hypothermia if proper precautions are not taken (see pp. 128-132). Physical exertion in cold weather can quickly lead to exhaustion, muscle fatigue, and chills due to overheating and subsequent cooling. Make sure that you follow these preventive measures:

☐ Wear several layers of clothing. You can remove each one as you get warmer with exercise. Fabrics should be loosely woven to allow water vapor from your skin to escape.

☐ Keep the head and hands covered and warm to prevent greatest heat loss.

■ LIGHTNING

If you are outside when a lightning storm hits, do the following:

☐ Stay away from water, ridges, and solitary trees, and don't touch metal.

☐ Get into a hollow or ditch and crouch down under brush if possible—unless it's wet there.

☐ Get inside a building or car as soon as possible.

MENTAL HEALTH

Living or traveling in the developing world can temporarily disrupt your mental well-being. Initially, you may experience feelings of loneliness as a result of being separated from friends and family. These feelings are compounded by a lack of familiarity with your new environment. Different languages, food, weather, pace of life, and cultural practices can overwhelm the newcomer and cause a feeling of disorientation. The physical sickness that often accompanies adjustment to a new environment can add to your mental discomfort. On an interpersonal level, although you may be meeting individuals who welcome and support you, the newness of these relationships and their lack of "depth" can make them feel unsatisfying. Additionally, it may feel strange to have lost your anonymity and always be the "outsider."

For individuals who are in developing countries to work for an extended period of time, a sense of frustration may result from an initial inability to be effective. Before departure, one anticipates great possibilities for the pending adventure. On arriving, however, language barriers and an unfamiliarity with social patterns delay one's ability to contribute.

How to best overcome these difficulties is obviously situation- and individual-specific. Perhaps most important is the knowledge that these feelings of depression or loneliness are common and almost always temporary. Be patient with your situation and yourself by releasing unrealistic expectations. The transition into your new lifestyle may take awhile, but try to enjoy and learn through the challenge it presents.

Studying the local language, taking walks, reading, writing, playing an instrument, exercising, participating in a cultural activity, or taking pictures will enable you to explore your new environment in a positive and productive manner. It is equally important to share your feelings with another person, even if it is through letters. Traveling and living in the Third World may be emotionally stressful at times, but the rewards in personal growth and experience can, in the end, far exceed the initial difficulties.

Guidelines For Diagnosis And Treatment Of Illness

Even if you follow all of the preventive measures outlined in the previous chapters, you still may find yourself or a friend sick at some time during your stay.

This chapter gives guidelines to diagnosing and treating illness. Included are the signs to watch for in a person who is sick or injured, signs of dangerous illness, and guidelines for the correct use of medicine. Review and refer to these guidelines whenever someone is sick.

SIGNS TO WATCH FOR

Monitor the temperature, breathing, pulse, and eyes of yourself or someone else who is sick or injured.

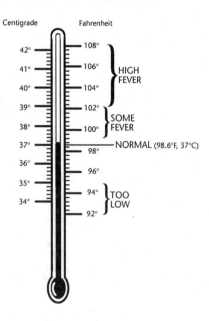

■ TEMPERATURE

Taking a sick person's temperature is wise, even if that person does not seem to have a fever. If the person is very sick, take the temperature at least 4 times each day and write it down.

It is important to find out when and how the fever comes, how long it lasts, and how it goes away. This may help you identify the disease. For example:

☐ Malaria usually causes high fever attacks that begin with chills, last a few hours, and may come back every 2 or 3 days (see pp. 80-81).

☐ Typhoid causes a fever that rises a little more every day (see pp. 77-79).

There are two kinds of thermometer scales, Centigrade (C) and Fahrenheit (F). Either can be used to measure a person's temperature. See illustration on the previous page.

■ BREATHING (RESPIRATION)

Note the way the sick person breathes—the depth (deep or shallow), rate (how often the breaths are taken), and the difficulty. Notice if both sides of the chest move equally as the person breathes.

Use a watch or clock to count the number of breaths per minute. Between 12 and 20 breaths per minute is normal for adults and older children. Up to 30 breaths per minute is normal for children, and 40 for babies. People with a high fever or serious respiratory illness (like pneumonia) breathe more quickly than normal. More than 40 shallow breaths a minute usually indicates pneumonia.

■ PULSE (HEARTBEAT)

Note the strength, the rate, and the regularity of the pulse. Use a watch or clock to count the pulses per minute.

The pulse gets much faster with exercise and when and when a person is nervous, frightened, or has a fever. As a general rule, the pulse in-

NORMAL PULSE FOR PEOPLE AT REST

adults . . 60 to 80 beats per minute

children . . . . 80 to 100

babies . . . . 100 to 140

creases 20 beats per minute for a rise in fever of one degree Centigrade (1°C) or two degrees Fahrenheit (2°F).

To take a person's pulse, put your fingers on the wrist as shown. (Do not use your thumb to feel for the pulse.)

If you cannot find the pulse in the wrist, feel for it in the neck beside the voicebox . . .

or put your ear directly on the chest and listen for the heartbeat, or use a stethoscope if you have one.

When a person is very ill, take the pulse often and write it down along with the temperature and rate of breathing.

It is important to notice changes in the pulse rate. For example:

☐ A weak, rapid pulse can mean a state of shock (see pp. 144-145).

☐ A very rapid, very slow, or irregular pulse could mean heart trouble.

☐ A relatively slow pulse in a person with a high fever may be a sign of typhoid (see pp. 77-79).

■ EYES

Look at the color of the white part of the eyes. Is it normal, red, or yellow? Also note any changes in the sick person's vision.

Pay attention to the size of the pupils. If they are very large, it can mean a state of shock (see pp. 144-145). If they are very small, it can mean poison or the effect of certain drugs.

A big difference in the size of the pupils is almost always a medical emergency. Difference in the size of the pupils (i.e., left eye compared to right eye) of an unconscious person who has had a recent head injury may mean brain damage.

Always compare the two pupils of a person who is unconscious or has had a head injury.

SIGNS OF DANGEROUS ILLNESS

Someone who has one or more of the following signs is probably too sick to be treated without skilled medical help. The person's life may be in danger. **Seek medical help as soon as possible.**

☐ Loss of large amounts of blood from anywhere in the body (see pp. 138-139).

☐ Coughing up blood.

☐ Marked blueness of lips and nails.

☐ Great difficulty in breathing which does not improve with rest.

☐ The person cannot be wakened (coma) (see pp. 142-144).

☐ The person is so weak he faints when he stands up.

☐ A day or more without being able to urinate.

☐ A day or more without being able to drink any liquids (see pp. 49-50).

☐ Heavy vomiting or severe diarrhea that lasts for more than 1 day in an adult or more than a few hours in babies (see pp. 50-51).

☐ Blood or mucus in the stools.

☐ Black stools like tar, or vomit with blood or feces.

☐ Strong, continuous stomach pains with vomiting in a person who does not have diarrhea or cannot have a bowel movement (see pp. 147-149).

☐ Any strong continuous pain that lasts for more than 3 days.

☐ Stiff neck with arched back, with or without a stiff jaw.

☐ Convulsions in someone with fever or serious illness (see pp. 150-151).

☐ High fever (above 102°F or 39°C) that cannot be brought down or that lasts more than 4 or 5 days (see pp. 150-151).

☐ Weight loss over an extended period of time.

☐ Blood in the urine (see pp. 97-98).

☐ Sores that keep growing and do not go away with treatment.

☐ A lump, in any part of the body, that keeps getting bigger.

☐ Lack of feeling in an extremity due to cold (see pp. 129-131).

☐ Severe illnesses at high altitude (see p. 137).

GUIDELINES FOR THE USE OF MEDICINES

☐ Use medicines only when necessary.

☐ Know the correct use and precautions for any medicine you use.

☐ Be sure to use the right dose.

☐ If the medicine does not help, or causes problems, stop using it.

☐ When in doubt, seek the advice of a health professional.

Note: Some health workers and doctors give medicines when none are needed, often because they think patients expect medicine and will not be satisfied unless they get some. Tell your doctor or health worker you only want medicine if it is definitely needed.

TAKING MEDICINES ON A FULL OR EMPTY STOMACH

Some medicines work best when you take them on an empty stomach—that is, one hour before meals. Other medicines are less likely to cause upset stomach or heartburn when taken along with a meal or right afterwards.

Take these medicines 1 hour before or 2 hours after meals:

☐ penicillin

☐ ampicillin

☐ tetracycline (take with plenty of water and avoid dairy products)

Take these medicines together with or soon after meals:

☐ aspirin and medicines that contain aspirin

☐ iron (ferrous sulfate)

☐ vitamins

☐ erythromycin (an alternative to penicillin for those allergic to penicillin)

Antacids do the most good if you take them when the stomach is empty, 1 or 2 hours after meals and at bedtime.

Alcohol combined with antihistamines causes excessive drowsiness—obviously hazardous if you are driving a car or motorcycle, for example. The best rule is to avoid alcohol whenever you have taken medication.

Caution: Remember that there is some danger in the use of any medicine. Whenever you take a drug, you are balancing the dangers of the disease or condition you are treating against the drug's possible side effects.

■ ANTIBIOTICS

GUIDELINES FOR THE USE OF ANTIBIOTICS

☐ If you do not know exactly how to use the antibiotic and what infections it can be used for, do not use it.

☐ Use only an antibiotic that is recommended for the infection you wish to treat.

☐ Use the antibiotic only in the recommended dose—no more, no less. The dose depends on the illness and the age or weight of the sick person.

☐ Keep using the antibiotics for the recommended number of days or 2 days after the fever and other signs of infection are gone in order to make sure the illness is completely cured. Do not take antibiotics sporadically.

☐ If the antibiotic causes skin rash, itching, difficult breathing, or any serious reactions, stop using it and consult a doctor about a possible allergy to the antibiotic.

WHAT TO DO IF AN ANTIBIOTIC DOES NOT SEEM TO HELP

For most common infections, antibiotics begin to bring improvement in a day or two. If the antibiotic you are using does not bring any improvement, it is possible that:

☐ The illness is not what you think. Try to find out exactly what the illness is.

☐ You may be using the wrong medicine. Check it.

☐ The dose of the antibiotic is not correct. Check it.

☐ The bacteria have become resistant to the antibiotic being used and are thus no longer harmed by it. Try another one of the antibiotics recommended for that illness.

☐ You may not know enough to cure the illness. Get medical help, especially if the condition is serious or getting worse.

IMPORTANCE OF LIMITED USE OF ANTIBIOTICS

The use of all medicines should be limited. But this is especially true of antibiotics, for the following reasons:

☐ **Allergic reactions.** Antibiotics not only kill bacteria, they can also harm the body by causing allergic reactions. Many people die each year due to allergic reactions to antibiotics.

☐ **Upsetting the natural balance.** Not all bacteria in the body are harmful. Some are necessary for the body to function normally. Antibiotics often kill the good bacteria along with the harmful ones. Antibiotics may kill some kinds of bacteria necessary for digestion, upsetting the natural balance of bacteria in the gut. Thus, persons who take ampicillin and other broad-spectrum antibiotics for several days may develop diarrhea.

☐ **Resistance to treatment.** When attacked many times by the same antibiotic, bacteria become resistant and are no longer killed by it. For this reason, certain dangerous diseases like typhoid are becoming more difficult to treat than they were a few years ago. Throughout the world important diseases are becoming resistant to antibiotics—largely because antibiotics are used too much for minor infections.

For most minor infections, antibiotics are not needed and should not be used. Minor skin infections can usually be successfully treated with soap and water and hot soaks. Minor respiratory infections are best treated by drinking lots of liquids, eating good food, and getting plenty of rest. For most diarrheas, antibiotics are not necessary and may even be harmful.

Do not use antibiotics for infections the body can fight successfully by itself. Save them for when they are needed.

BUYING MEDICATIONS IN DEVELOPING COUNTRIES

In many countries, there are fewer restrictions than in the U.S. on types of medicines that can be sold over the counter—you may not need a prescription to buy antibiotics, malaria pills, and other drugs. This can be useful if you know exactly what your problem is and what drug you need. But be aware that self-diagnosis and treatment involve risks, especially when strong drugs are used. Potentially dangerous drugs such as chloramphenicol (which can be lethal), butazolidin, and aminopyrine may be found in cold and fever remedies or prescribed for nonspecific illnesses in some countries.

If you do buy drugs over the counter that would require a prescription in the U.S.:

☐ Know the generic name; be sure of what you are getting.

☐ Talk with your doctor at home first about antibiotics or other drugs you might possibly need. Know how to use them and be aware of possible side effects.

☐ Follow the guidelines for the use of medicines and antibiotics given above.

If you need to get an injection, be sure that the syringe and needle have been sterilized. When in doubt about standards of cleanliness, buy your own needle and syringe and bring it with you to the doctor's office or clinic.

FOLK REMEDIES

You are likely to encounter folk remedies using foods, teas, herbal medicines, and so on for many health problems. Use your common sense to evaluate such remedies. If you feel fairly certain that no harm can come from them, give them a try. They often work.

GETTING MEDICAL CARE

The availability and quality of medical care in the developing world varies widely from region to region, and of course, among individual hospitals, doctors, and health workers. Familiarize yourself with local facilities and medical practices **before** you need them. Know what steps you will take if you find yourself suddenly ill or in need of help.

Sources of information on doctors and medical care can be obtained overseas through:

☐ The U.S. Embassy or Consulate

☐ American residents in the area

☐ Overseas offices of international corporations

☐ The American Chamber of Commerce

☐ Peace Corps offices

☐ Hotel managers in hotels that cater to tourists

☐ Tourist information centers and tourist brochures

☐ Travel services like American Express, Cooks, etc.

☐ Airlines

☐ University-affiliated or missionary hospitals

☐ The telephone book

☐ Local police

☐ The provincial health office

Though many people speak English in cities, it is still a good idea to learn how to say "I need a doctor" in the local language. The organization IAMAT has already been mentioned (see p. 20) as a good source of information on English-speaking doctors.

It is a good idea to carry identification *at all times* with instructions in the local language. This information should include the address and phone number of a local contact, the phone number of your embassy or consulate, your passport number, and the name of a person in the U.S. (or wherever home is) to contact in case of an emergency. Carrying this information can be important if, for example, you are in a motorcycle or bus accident that leaves you injured or unconscious and unable to personally make decisions about medical treatment.

In other countries, attitudes and expectations about health care will sometimes differ from your own. (One American volunteer, hospitalized in a large Indonesian city, discovered that the hospital food mainly consisted of rice porridge—it was assumed that family or friends would bring other food for the patients.) For reassurance or answers to questions of this kind, ask a local friend or contact your embassy or consulate.

■ IF YOU ARE FAR FROM A MEDICAL FACILITY

If you are living or spending time far from a medical facility, you will want to be prepared for medical emergencies. In such situations, it is especially important that you have gathered together and know how to use appropriate medical supplies before you need them. See pp. 15-19 for a partial list of supplies you might need.

Determine the potential dangers in your area and know how to treat them. For example, if you are in an area that has poisonous snakes and you are more than 12 hours from a medical facility, the basic first-aid steps for a snakebite described on pp. 167-168 may be insufficient. Know about the snakes in your area and perhaps even keep a dose of antivenin available. Obviously, you should not diagnose and treat illnesses or injuries unless it is an emergency and you are sure of what you are doing.

Common Health Problems

The following is a discussion of the most common health ailments and concerns of people spending time in less-developed regions of the world. Use this chapter to familiarize yourself with the problems you are most likely to face and as an introduction to the more detailed "Infections and Diseases" chapter that follows.

DEHYDRATION

Dehydration is an excessive loss of body fluids and is caused by such things as diarrhea, vomiting, heat and humidity, heavy work, and high altitude.

The **signs of dehydration** include: little or no urination, dark yellow urine, headache, and dry mouth and eyes. Urine output of less than 2 cups per 24 hours indicates dehydration. In serious cases, one may have difficulty breathing, nausea, dizziness, numbness, and increased body temperature. A test for dehydration is to pinch a small amount of skin on the soft part of the forearm, hold it for a second, and then let go. If the skin falls down slowly instead of popping down instantly, you're dehydrated.

Avoid dehydration by drinking lots of liquids. If there is a danger of dehydration, use pre-mixed "oral rehydration solution" packets or the "rehydration drink formula" described below. This formula helps to replace the fluid and salts (sodium, potassium, chloride, and bicarbonate) that are being lost through diarrheal fluid, vomiting, respiration, and/or sweat. If the ingredients for this formula are not immediately obtainable, drink whatever liquid is available! **Do not delay**; it is critically important that you consume adequate amounts of liquid to prevent serious illness.

Note: If you are dehydrated and purified water is unavailable, **drink whatever liquid is at hand**, even if it might be contaminated.

Avoiding or treating severe dehydration is usually worth the risk.

REHYDRATION DRINK FORMULA

1 quart (4 cups or 1 liter) of boiled **water** or diluted **fruit juice**
(fruit juice provides potassium; orange, lemon, or apple juice
are recommended)

2 tablespoons **sugar** or **honey**

$1/4$ teaspoon **salt**

$1/4$ teaspoon **baking soda** (if you don't have soda, use another $1/4$
teaspoon salt)

Caution: Before using the formula, taste it; make sure it is no
saltier than tears.

DIARRHEA

Even if you follow the recommended precautions for eating and
drinking, you're likely to have at least a few bouts with diarrhea.
Often, traveler's diarrhea is your body's way of adjusting to a new
type of intestinal bacteria. It can also be the result of changing one's
normal sleep cycle (due to jet lag) and eating habits, or of emotional
stress associated with travel.

A simple case of diarrhea usually goes away in a day or two. **The
greatest danger with diarrhea is dehydration due to lost body fluids
and salts** (this is especially dangerous for children). The onset of dehydration is rapid if diarrhea is accompanied by vomiting. If you have
diarrhea, it is critical that you drink plenty of fluids, preferably in the
form of the "rehydration drink formula" described above. For a detailed discussion of how you should care for yourself when you have simple diarrhea and the medications used to treat diarrhea, see pp. 60-63.

SEEK MEDICAL HELP FOR DIARRHEA IF:

☐ Diarrhea is accompanied by a fever higher than 101°F (38.3°C)
or if a slightly lower fever persists for more than 24 hours.

□ Diarrhea lasts more than 4 days and is not getting better (or more than 1 day in a small child with severe diarrhea).

□ You were very sick, weak, or malnourished before the diarrhea began.

□ You are becoming increasingly dehydrated.

□ There is vomiting for more than 6-12 hours in addition to diarrhea.

□ There is blood or mucus in the stools.

□ You have "explosive" diarrhea or yellow diarrhea with froth (see p. 66).

VOMITING

Vomiting has various causes: a bacterial or viral infection of the intestines, poisoning from spoiled food, motion sickness, high-altitude sickness, or almost any illness with high fever or severe pain. As with diarrhea, the greatest danger is that of dehydration. Take small sips of carbonated drinks, tea, or the rehydration drink described above. Don't eat anything while vomiting is severe. If vomiting does not stop, take a medicine like promethizine (25-50 mg twice a day).

DANGER SIGNS WITH VOMITING—GET MEDICAL HELP QUICKLY

□ Increasing dehydration that you can't control.

□ Severe vomiting that lasts more than 24 hours.

□ Violent vomiting, especially if vomit is dark green, brown, or smells like feces.

□ Constant pain in the abdomen, especially if you can't defecate, or if someone putting an ear to your abdomen can't hear gurgles (see "appendicitis," pp. 148-149).

□ Vomiting of, or with, blood.

FEVER

Fever can be a sign of many different illnesses. Fever often accompanies a bout of the flu and is one of the main signs of diseases like malaria and typhoid. Use a thermometer to monitor temperature (see pp. 38-39) since different diseases show different fever patterns. If you suffer from a high fever that you think might be caused by a serious disease, get medical attention. See chapter 6 for a discussion of diseases that cause fever.

Whenever you have a fever, wear as little clothing as possible, take aspirin to lower the fever, and **drink lots of cool liquids** to replace the fluid that is lost through the skin. For additional treatment of fever, see pp. 77-78.

SKIN AND HAIR PROBLEMS

■ SUNBURN

Under certain conditions (e.g., in the tropics, at the ocean, and at high altitude), **sunburn** occurs quickly, especially if you are not already tan or protected by a sunscreen lotion.

Avoid sunburn by limiting your exposure to 20 minutes a day at first, gradually increasing this time as you acquire a tan. Use sunscreen lotions liberally and reapply after swimming or heavy sweating. Sunscreen lotions containing para-aminobenzoic acid (PABA) or oxybenzone are most effective; get one with a high (greater than "10") blocking rating. Remember, a high percentage of the sun's rays are reflected off sand, water, and snow. Be sure to put sunscreen on your ears and the underside of your nose even if you are wearing a hat.

Some things to remember about the sun and sunburn: since many of the sun's rays penetrate cloud cover, you can still get sunburned on overcast days. Also, ultraviolet rays can penetrate thin clothing. Many medications (such as tetracycline and sulfas) cause the skin to be especially sensitive to sunburn. When you are out in the sun, be cautioned that the full degree of sunburn does not show until several hours after exposure.

If you get sunburned, use cold compresses and take aspirin (or *Tylenol*) to relieve the pain and reduce the swelling. Calamine lotion is good for minor sunburn. Severe sunburn, especially when it leads to blistered skin, requires medical attention.

The sun's rays are also harmful to your eyes. Protect your eyes by wearing dark, preferably mirrored, sunglasses and a hat. Beware of cheap, "fashion" sunglasses that have little or no protective capacity.

■ FUNGUS INFECTIONS

The heat, humidity, and less-hygienic conditions of the tropics are conducive to fungus infections. These infections are one of the most common ailments of visitors and should be guarded against. Keep as clean and dry as possible and use baby powder. Wear loose, breathable clothes and change them often (see p. 19).

■ SKIN INFECTIONS

Take special care of any wound, however small. In the tropics, tiny scrapes and cuts become easily and painfully infected if they are not kept clean and covered (see pp. 153-157).

■ ALLERGIC REACTIONS

You may find that you have an allergic reaction to a new substance that your body encounters in the Third World. If you suffer from unexplained rashes or hives, try to determine whether they are caused by a certain food or substance (e.g., people have found that they react to some laundry soaps used in the developing world). To relieve itching, use cool water, a baking soda and water solution, or calamine lotion. If the allergic reaction is severe, take an antihistamine like chlorpheniramine. Dimenhydrinate (*Dramamine*), usually sold for motion sickness, may help.

■ HAIR LOSS

Hair loss in quantities greater than normal is often seen in long-term residents in developing countries.

Sudden hair loss can sometimes follow high fevers, inflammatory skin disorders, sudden and excessive weight loss, severe anemia, change in diet, and intestinal disorders. If you suddenly lose large amounts of hair, one of these factors may be the cause. If so, this loss is usually **reversible** and your hair should fill back in with time.

FOR WOMEN

■ MENSTRUATION

It is likely that you will miss periods or have an irregular menstrual cycle while overseas. Some women have gone several months without a period. Irregularities like this are fairly normal considering the change of environment and shouldn't be cause for concern (unless, of course, you are pregnant). Symptoms of premenstrual syndrome (PMS) may also change overseas, due to your new diet and environment.

Sanitary napkins are available in most towns and cities, but not in the more remote areas. Tampons are rare and expensive. Keep track of your periods so you won't be caught unprepared while on a trip to a remote area.

There may be local customs regarding menstruation. For example, in some Hindu cultures menstruating women are not allowed to enter temples. Ask local women if there are any customs you should observe. Also, in areas where water is plentiful and used in place of toilet paper (see p. 26), soiled napkins and tampons are rinsed clean and then disposed of. This is easy and practical in such areas, where toilet paper is rare and where such items should not be introduced into the sewage system.

■ CONTRACEPTION

If you plan to use contraception while overseas, bring with you whatever supplies you'll need, or plan to have them sent to you. It may be difficult or impossible to find the particular kind of contraception you want. (Also, in some societies, distribution of contraception is limited to those who are married.) Consult a gynecologist or family planning clinic before you leave to determine the most appropriate form of contraception for you and to obtain what you'll need while overseas.

The Pill is available in most parts of the Third World, but it could be difficult to find a Pill with the particular combination or level of hormones that you are used to.

Vomiting and diarrhea can reduce the Pill's effectiveness by interfering with its absorption into the body. Some antibiotics may also interfere with its effectiveness. If you use the Pill, be sure to use a backup method of contraception in addition to the Pill during such times. If you'll be experiencing a major time change in your travels, consult your doctor about the best way to schedule your intake of the Pill.

Condoms are available in most developing countries. Diaphragms, jellies and foams are rare (or nonexistent). If you plan to use a diaphragm, keep in mind that heat and humidity will cause the rubber to break down more quickly than usual, and sanitary conditions may make it more difficult to keep the diaphragm adequately clean.

You may want to avoid the use of an intrauterine device (IUD) while spending an extended period of time in the Third World, since insertion and removal of the IUD, and treatment of any complications (infections, bleeding, embedding, etc.) must be done only by a well-trained person who has experience with IUDs, and may require use of X rays or ultrasound (which may not be readily available). Also, the IUD's string (which stays in the vagina) can carry bacteria from the vagina into the uterus, increasing your risk of infection.

■ BLADDER AND VAGINAL INFECTIONS

See pp. 95-101 for a complete discussion of vaginal and bladder (urinary tract) infections. You may be more susceptible to such infections while living or traveling abroad, due to changes in your diet and environment. If you know you tend to get a particular kind of infection, pay close attention to **preventive measures** and bring with you any appropriate medication. Pages 102-115 includea a discussion of sexually transmitted diseases.

Note: If you are being treated for any ongoing gynecological problems (such as endometriosis), bring with you whatever medication you'll need, since it may not be available in developing countries.

■ PREGNANCY

If you are pregnant, you **must** take special precautions when traveling overseas. There are restrictions on which immunizations, antibiotics, and other medications pregnant women should receive. If you must travel while pregnant, consult with your doctor.

OTHER PROBLEMS

■ CONSTIPATION

Individual bowel rhythms vary widely. Some people have 3 stools a day, while for others, one stool every 3 days is normal. Constipation can be caused by disruption of your normal schedule, eating habits (not eating enough fruit, green vegetables, or foods with natural fiber), not drinking enough liquids, or not getting enough exercise.

Usually, a change in diet or more exercise will be the only treatment needed. Take laxatives if you need to, but don't use them if you have stomach pain.

■ MOTION SICKNESS

Transportation is often rugged and uncomfortable in the Third World. If you are susceptible to motion sickness or anticipating a particularly "adventurous" overnight bus ride, there are a number of things you can do to avoid feeling sick.

Before and during travel, avoid spicy, fried, or fatty foods and alcohol. But do not stop eating altogether; it is best to keep small amounts of bland foods in your stomach, even if you feel nauseous. Also, drink plenty of liquids. Travel in loose, comfortable clothing.

Anti-motion sickness drugs (see p. 18) should be taken or applied (in the case of *Transderm Scop*) before travel, since they are much less effective once symptoms have developed. Many of these drugs cause drowsiness, so should be avoided if you are going to be in control of a vehicle. (**Caution:** Some drugs should not be taken by pregnant women or children.)

While traveling, sit in the front seats of buses and cars and in the middle sections of boats and planes (where movement is least), look straight ahead at the horizon in the direction of travel, sit in a reclined position or lie down if possible, and do not read.

■ HEAT ILLNESSES

The combination of high temperature and humidity, as well as the use of sunscreen lotion, limits the body's ability to cool itself and may result in a variety of heat illness.

Heat cramps and **heat exhaustion** are two health problems caused by heat. Generally, these are caused by a loss of salt and water due to overexertion and heavy sweating. To prevent them drink lots of fluids (including fruit juices and soups), try to avoid going out in the hottest part of the day, wear loose, breathable (cotton) clothing and a hat, and eat light meals, but avoid alcoholic beverages, which disrupt heat control mechanisms.

Warning signs of heat illnesses include: fatigue, dizziness, cramps, and headache. For additional signs and treatment, see pp. 125-127.

Heat rash is another common problem that is best prevented by wearing loose-fitting clothes, keeping dry, and using a powder after bathing.

■ WEIGHT FLUCTUATION

Weight fluctuation is common among long-term visitors in developing countries as they adjust to a new diet and environment. Gains or losses of 5-20 lbs (2-8 kg) are not unusual and should not be cause for alarm. Attention to diet and exercise will help to control weight. In general, body weight should stabilize over time or upon returning home to one's previous diet and lifestyle. If weight loss is severe (greater than 20 lbs), you may have worms or some other disease—get medical attention.

■ MOUNTAIN SICKNESS

If you are in the mountains above 10,000 feet (3,000 meters), there is a good chance you will suffer from some of the symptoms of mountain (altitude) sickness. There are a variety of forms of this sickness, but all can be avoided by gaining altitude *slowly* (see p. 133).

■ MOTORCYCLE ACCIDENTS

Motorcycle accidents, not malaria or typhoid, are the cause of the greatest number of fatalities among Peace Corps volunteers.

If you choose to ride a motorcycle, even as a passenger, **wear a helmet**. Make sure the helmet is high quality since many sold in the Third World are cheaply made and will not protect you. Also, wear heavy clothing (long pants and a jacket) and shoes in case of a fall. Do not ride in shorts and sandals. Drive safely!

Infections And Diseases

As a traveler or longer-term visitor in the Third World, you'll probably need to be more self-reliant in many ways—including maintaining your health. At home, if you have a health problem, it's relatively simple to go to a doctor or clinic, ask friends for advice, or check out a book from the library and do your own research. In another country, you may find health care a more complicated process. Your problem may be too minor to warrant a visit to the doctor, but you may not have access to written information about it or know anyone to ask. Other factors—for example, a language barrier, lack of funds, or social stigma attached to gynecological problems—can make it harder than usual to get prompt medical attention. You may find yourself needing information to help you decide what to do next. That's where we hope this chapter will help.

While not advocating self-diagnosis and treatment, we feel there are several valid arguments for providing reference information on diseases and health problems. 1) If your problem is a minor one, like heat rash or worms, having the necessary information allows you to handle it yourself or allays your fears until you can get medical attention. 2) If you don't know how serious your symptoms are, this chapter can help you decide whether or not you should see a doctor. 3) If you can't get to a doctor immediately, you can find out how to alleviate your symptoms in the meantime. 4) If you understand your body better, you may be able to offer relevant information that helps the doctor diagnose your problem. Or if you aren't confident about one doctor's diagnosis or treatment, you'll know better how to go about looking for a second opinion.

We hope that this chapter will give you an accurate outline of some problems you may encounter, but it can only be useful if you understand its limitations. It is **not** a complete medical reference, and whatever you gain from reading it is intended to complement, not replace, the knowledge and experience that a good doctor uses to treat illness.

■ HOW TO USE THIS CHAPTER

Even before you become ill, you may want to skim this chapter and note the various ways in which diseases can be transmitted. Do not, however, become overwhelmed by the number of diseases described here. Many are extremely rare and are included solely for the sake of completeness.

In this chapter, diseases or health problems are grouped roughly according to the system or part of the body that they affect. Pick out the group that relates to your symptoms, then see whether any of the illnesses described sounds like what you have. Be careful not to assume that you have a particular disease simply because you show some of the symptoms.

Some of the diseases described are found only in certain parts of the world. For these, a listing of the areas where the disease is common is included. If no specific geographic regions are listed, this indicates that the ailment is endemic throughout the most parts of the Third World.

Obviously, some diseases are more common than others. Included in the description of each ailment is whether the "risk of contracting" is very high, high, moderate, low, or extremely low. These distinctions are generalizations; locale and living conditions will greatly influence the likelihood of getting a certain ailment.

DIGESTIVE TRACT

■ DIARRHEA

Diarrhea is the most common ailment of travelers in Asia, Africa, and Latin America. It can be caused by various forms of bacteria and viruses, certain types of foods, food poisoning, and emotional stress. It can be dangerous since it may lead to severe dehydration.

RISK OF CONTRACTING: Very high.

PREVENTION AND TREATMENT:

- ☐ Observe the rules of hygiene.

- ☐ Avoid eating too many rich, fatty, highly spiced foods and fruits.

- ☐ Some drugs (*Pepto-Bismol,* trimethoprim/sulfamethoxazole, and doxycycline) may be used to prevent diarrhea if taken prophylactically (prior to getting sick). Though this regimen is somewhat effective, the U.S. Public Health Service does *not* recommend this practice for long-term travelers (greater than 3 weeks) in developing countries. Taking these drugs preventively increases the risks of side effects, is expensive, and, from a public health standpoint, will promote the emergence of drug-resistant bacteria.

DRINKING DURING DIARRHEA ATTACKS:

- ☐ With mild diarrhea, replace fluid losses by drinking water, carbonated drinks (caffeine-free is best) fruit juices, clear soups, and herbal teas.

- ☐ Drink 2 glasses of liquid after every trip to the bathroom; or if you are vomiting and can't keep large amounts of liquid down, take small sips every 5 minutes.

- ☐ For severe or continued diarrhea, oral-rehydration formulas (p. 50) are best for replacing the fluids and salts lost during the illness.

- ☐ An adult with diarrhea should drink 12 or more cups (3 quarts or liters) of liquid a day. A small child (under 80 lbs or 37 kg) needs at least 4 cups (1 liter) a day. Infants should continue breast-feeding and receiving pure water while taking the rehydration formula.

EATING DURING DIARRHEA ATTACKS:

- ☐ While replacing body fluids is important, well-nourished adults should **avoid solid foods** for the first 24 hours of a diarrhea attack.

- ☐ If the diarrhea lasts for more than one day, begin eating bland solid foods to supply energy and nutrients. Ripe or cooked bananas (also high in potassium), crackers, rice, and potatoes are good energy foods; lean meats and fish, boiled eggs, beans, lentils, and peas supply protein and vitamins.

☐ Avoid dairy products, raw vegetables, and fruits other than bananas since these tend to aggravate diarrhea. Also, avoid irritants to the digestive tract such as alcohol, caffeine, cocoa, cola beverages, spices, and fatty or greasy foods.

MEDICATIONS FOR DIARRHEA:

Often, your body will be able to overcome simple diarrhea without the use of drugs. If, however, the diarrhea does not subside after a couple of days or you "need" to stop the diarrhea (e.g., for a long bus ride), you may want to take some medication.

There are two categories of drugs that decrease diarrhea: **antidiarrheals**, which "plug you up" but do not attend to the underlying cause of the diarrhea and **antimicrobials**, which more directly attack the infective agent.

ANTIDIARRHEAL DRUGS:

☐ *Pepto-Bismol* (Bismuth-subsalicylate) is the best for mild or moderate diarrhea. *Pepto-Bismol* is available without a prescription and has few side effects (except in individuals who are taking salicylates [aspirin] for arthritis, or who are allergic to salicylate). Take 2-4 tablets every 30 minutes (for a maximum of 8 times per day) or, as a liquid, 1 oz (2 tablespoons) every 30 minutes (also for a maximum of 8 times per day). Use should be limited to a 48-hour period. Minor side effects of blackening of the tongue and stools are not cause for alarm.

☐ *Lomotil* and *Imodium* slow the movement of your intestines and thus decrease diarrhea. They also relieve cramping. However, these drugs can be **potentially dangerous in severe diarrhea** since they mask fluid loss and retain the bacteria or infection that is causing the diarrhea rather than letting your body flush it out. Therefore, never use these medicines if you have any of the signs of a dangerous illness (see pp. 41-42). If these medications are not effective within 48 hours, you should discontinue their use and seek an alternative treatment. These drugs should not be used in children under age 2.

ANTIMICROBIAL DRUGS:

Antimicrobials (also called antibacterials) attack the cause of bacterial diarrhea and should be used only after waiting a day or so to see if the diarrhea will clear up itself (or if you show signs of a serious illness, e.g., fever, blood in stools). These drugs are quite powerful and therefore best used under the supervision of a trained medical person. If medical help is not immediately available, you may want to use an antidiarrheal drug until you can get qualified help. The most effective antimicrobial agents are:

☐ Trimethoprim/sulfamethoxazole (*Bactrim, Septra,* or cheaper generic brands). Normal dosage is 1 double-strength tablet (160 mg/800 mg) twice daily for 3 days.

☐ Doxycycline, 100 mg (1 tablet) twice daily for 3 days. (An alternate to doxycycline is tetracycline; 250 mg 4 times a day for 3 days).

☐ Ciprofloxicin, 500 mg, twice a day for 3 days.

Caution: All of these drugs have possible side effects, most commonly an increased sensitivity to sunlight. If you are taking these medications, you will burn more quickly and more severely than normal.

DRUGS TO AVOID:

A number of over-the-counter antidiarrheal drugs readily available in some developing countries **should be avoided** since they are potentially dangerous; these include:

☐ *Enterovioform, Mexaform.* Can cause neurological and optical damage.

☐ Chloramphenicol (*Chloromycetin*). Must be used under medical supervision.

☐ Mixtures containing neomycin and streptomycin. These can irritate the intestines.

■ AMOEBIC DYSENTERY

Caution: Diarrhea with blood may be either amoebic or bacillary (bacterial) dysentery (see next page). Usually, diarrhea with blood but no fever is caused by amoebas. Diarrhea with blood and fever is usually caused by a bacterial infection. The treatment of these two forms is different. A stool analysis is necessary in order to determine the cause of the diarrhea.

Amoebic dysentery should be treated properly, because relapses are common and the infection can later lead to inflammation or abscess of the liver.

RISK OF CONTRACTING: Low-moderate.

TRANSMISSION: Fecal-oral (through contaminated water or food).

PREVENTION: Observe the rules of hygiene (see pp. 23-27). Eating a balanced diet and avoiding fatigue also help.

SYMPTOMS:

- ☐ Diarrhea that comes and goes—sometimes alternating with constipation.

- ☐ Abdominal cramps and the need to have frequent bowel movements, even when little or nothing (or just mucus) comes out.

- ☐ Many loose (but usually not watery) stools with lots of mucus, sometimes with blood.

- ☐ In severe cases, the stools contain a lot of blood, you may feel very weak and ill.

- ☐ Usually no fever.

TREATMENT:

- ☐ Prevent dehydration with rehydration drink (see p. 50) and other fluids.

- ☐ Get medical attention and a stool analysis.

- ☐ Rest in bed, drink plenty of fluids, eat an easily digested diet that is rich in protein and vitamins.

☐ If medical care is unavailable, amoebic dysentery can be treated with metronidazole (*Flagyl*), 500-750 mg 3 times a day for 10 days. Do not drink alcohol while taking metronidazole.

■ BACILLARY DYSENTERY (SHIGELOSIS)

Caution: Diarrhea with blood may be either amoebic (see above) or bacillary (bacterial) dysentery. Usually, diarrhea with blood but no fever is caused by amoebas. Diarrhea with blood and fever is usually caused by a bacterial infection. The treatment of these two forms is different. A stool analysis is necessary in order to determine the cause of the diarrhea.

Bacillary dysentery is rarely dangerous. It will usually subside without medication after a week's time; medical treatment shortens this period.

RISK OF CONTRACTING: Low-moderate.

TRANSMISSION: Fecal-oral.

PREVENTION: Observe the rules of hygiene (see pp. 23-27). Eating a balanced diet and avoiding fatigue also helps.

SYMPTOMS:

☐ Sudden onset of watery diarrhea with blood or mucus.

☐ Fever (usually), ranging from 100° to 102°F (37.6° to 38.3°C).

☐ Abdominal cramps and the need to have frequent bowel movements, even if only blood and mucus come out.

TREATMENT:

☐ Prevent dehydration with rehydration drink (see p. 50) and other fluids.

☐ Get medical attention and a stool analysis.

☐ Rest in bed, drink plenty of fluids, eat an easily digested diet that is rich in protein and vitamins.

☐ If medical care is unavailable, bacillary dysentery can be treated with trimethoprim/sulfamethoxazole (*Bactrim, Septra*) one double-strength tablet (160 mg/800 mg) twice a day for 5 days. If allergic to sulfamides, substitute ciprofloxacin, 500 mg, twice a day for 5 days.

■ GIARDIA

Giardia is a microscopic parasite, like the amoeba, that lives in the intestines and is a common cause of diarrhea.

RISK OF CONTRACTING: Low-moderate.

TRANSMISSION: Fecal-oral.

PREVENTION: Observe the rules of hygiene.

SYMPTOMS:

☐ Yellow, bad-smelling diarrhea with bubbles or froth, but without blood or mucus.

☐ Uncomfortable, swollen abdomen.

☐ Mild cramps and lots of gas.

☐ Usually no fever.

TREATMENT:

☐ Giardia infections may clear up by themselves. Plenty of liquids, nutritious food, and rest are often the only treatment needed.

☐ Giardia is usually treated with metronidazole (*Flagyl*), 250 mg 3 times a day for 5 days or tinidazole (*Fasigyn*), 2 gm single dose. (Do not drink alcohol while taking metronidazole.) The drug quinacrine (*Atabrine*) works better, but can cause more side effects.

■ CHOLERA

Cholera is an intestinal disease that in the most severe cases causes rapid and extreme dehydration. The infection can also be mild or subclinical (without signs). Cholera has recently (January, 1991) been re-introduced into Latin America where it is currently (November, 1992) at epidemic levels in Peru, Ecuador, Columbia, and Bolivia and has been reported in almost every Central and South American country. In Peru, contaminated municipal water supplies have been implicated for the rapid spread of the disease.

RISK OF CONTRACTING: Low-moderate.

TRANSMISSION: Fecal-oral.

PREVENTION:
- ☐ The cholera vaccination is only 50% effective and not normally recommended by the CDC.

- ☐ Observe the rules of hygiene.

- ☐ In South America where cholera is a problem, avoid consuming water from the municipal water supplies.

- ☐ Raw and undercooked seafood, cold seafood salad, and peeled fruits should be particularly avoided.

SYMPTOMS:
- ☐ Sudden onset of acute diarrhea with "rice water" stools.

- ☐ Vomiting.

- ☐ Muscular cramps.

- ☐ Extreme weakness.

TREATMENT:
- ☐ Get medical help.

- ☐ Treat for dehydration, which is usually extreme, especially if there is vomiting with the diarrhea (see pp. 49-50).

- ☐ Get to a hospital as soon as possible. But if this cannot be accomplished immediately, take tetracycline, 4 500-mg capsules, 4 times a day for 5 days, or take erythromycin 500 mg 4 times a day for 3 days.

■ INTESTINAL WORMS

ROUNDWORM (ASCARIASIS)

Roundworms are spread through contaminated food or water. Once swallowed, the eggs hatch and the worms enter the bloodstream, which may cause general itching. The young worms then travel to the lungs, sometimes causing a dry cough, or, at worst, pneumonia with coughing of blood. The worms reach the intestines, where they grow to full size. They have a lifespan of 2-3 years.

RISK OF CONTRACTING: Moderate.

TRANSMISSION: Fecal-oral.

DESCRIPTION: 8-12 inches (20-30 cm) long. Color: pink or white. Appearance similar to an earthworm.

PREVENTION: Observe the rules of hygiene.

SYMPTOMS:
 □ May be vague abdominal discomfort.

TREATMENT:
 □ Treatment is with mebendozole, *Vermox* (100 mg, 2 times a day for 3 days **or** as a single dose of 500 mg) **or** with albendazole (single dose of 400 mg).

THREADWORM (PINWORM, ENTEROBIASIS)

(Most common in children.)

RISK OF CONTRACTING: Moderate.

TRANSMISSION: Fecal-oral. Once you have them, the worms lay thousands of eggs just outside the anus, which cause itching. If you scratch, the eggs stick under your fingernails and are carried to food and other objects, which causes other people to get infected.

DESCRIPTION: 1 cm long. Color: white. Very thin and threadlike.

PREVENTION: Observe the rules of hygiene.

SYMPTOMS:

- ☐ Itching in the anal region.

- ☐ Seeing a worm in your stools.

TREATMENT:

- ☐ Keep very clean; keep your fingernails short.

- ☐ Get a prescription from a doctor for medicine to get rid of the worms (often, 1 dose of mebendazole [100 mg] repeated after 2 weeks). It's a good idea to treat the whole household if one person has these worms.

- ☐ Even without medicine, if you carefully follow the rules of hygiene, most of the worms will be gone within a few weeks. Pinworms only live for about 6 weeks.

TAPEWORM

Tapeworm is an infection of the intestines caused by parasites found in animal flesh. If these parasites are eaten by people, they can grow up to several yards (meters) long.

RISK OF CONTRACTING: Low.

TRANSMISSION: Eating undercooked pork, beef, or fish that is infected.

SYMPTOMS:

- ☐ Symptoms are usually mild; they include a slight stomachache, loss of appetite, diarrhea, and weakness.

- ☐ Occasionally, a segment of the tapeworm will break loose and be found in the feces or underwear.

TREATMENT:

- ☐ Obtain medical treatment.

- ☐ Niclosamide (*Yomesan*) is the best drug for treating tapeworm, but should be taken under medical supervision.

HYDATID DISEASE (HYDATID CYST, ECHINOCOCCOSIS)

(Found primarily in Mexico and Central and South America)
This is a tapeworm disease of dogs, but people can become infected

by the larval stage of the worm. The disease is most prevalent in temperate and semitropical sheep-raising areas.

RISK OF CONTRACTING: Low.

TRANSMISSION: Ingesting the eggs of the tapeworms. This can occur by consuming food or water that has been contaminated with dog feces, or by touching an infected dog and then placing fingers in the mouth. The latter is the usual mode of transmission for children.

PREVENTION:
- ☐ Observe the rules of hygiene.
- ☐ Wash your hands after touching potentially infected dogs.
- ☐ Regular worming of dogs.

SYMPTOMS:
- ☐ Usually, there are no symptoms.
- ☐ After many decades, the cysts (usually found in the liver) produce abdominal pain.
- ☐ Chest X rays and other medical tests may determine infection before there are symptoms.

TREATMENT:
- ☐ Obtain medical care.

TRICHINOSIS

Trichinosis worms are never seen in the stools. They burrow through the person's intestines and get into the muscles.

RISK OF CONTRACTING: Moderate.

TRANSMISSION: Eating undercooked pork that is infected.

PREVENTION: Eat pork only if it has been well cooked.

SYMPTOMS:
- ☐ Diarrhea and nausea a few hours to 5 days after eating the infected meat.

☐ Later, fever with chills and muscle pain.

TREATMENT:

☐ Seek medical help at once.

☐ Thiabendazole may help, but it should be taken under medical supervision.

OTHER WORMS

A number of other worms found in the Third World have not been described in detail here because they aren't likely to be a problem for travelers or visitors. Hookworms live in the soil and enter the body through a person's bare feet—so always wear shoes as an essential preventive measure. Guinea worms (*Dracunculus medinensis*) are transmitted to people when infected shellfish are eaten raw or partially cooked. Guinea worms are a problem in Africa, northern South America and south Asia.

MEDICINES FOR WORMING

Caution: These should only be taken under the supervision of a medical professional.

FOR HOOKWORM, WHIPWORM, ROUNDWORM, AND THREADWORM:

☐ Mebendozole (*Vermox*) is one of the best drugs. Dosage: 1 100-mg tablet, twice daily for 3 days (6 tablets total) **or** as a single dose of 500 mg. **Alternately,** albendazole as a single dose of 400 mg.

FOR TAPEWORM:

☐ Niclosamide (*Yomesan*) is best. See package for dosage.

SKIN

Many skin problems require specific treatment, but here are two general rules that often help.

☐ If the affected area is hot and painful, treat it with heat. Put warm, moist cloths on it.

☐ If the affected area itches, stings, or oozes, treat it with cold. Put cool, wet cloths on it (cold compresses).

■ SUNBURN

For a complete discussion of sunburn, see p. 52.

PREVENTION:

☐ Limit your exposure.

☐ Use sunscreen lotions containing high concentrations of para-aminobenzoic acid (PABA) liberally.

TREATMENT:

☐ Use cold compresses to relieve itching and swelling.

☐ Take aspirin for pain.

☐ Severe sunburn, including blistered skin, requires medical attention.

■ FUNGUS INFECTIONS

Fungus infections occur most frequently in 4 areas of the body: on the scalp (tinea capitis); on the body (ringworm); between the toes or fingers (athlete's foot); and in the groin (jock itch or crotch rot).

Fungus infections thrive in a warm, moist environment. Perspiration and tight clothing add to the problem.

Note: Ringworm is not caused by a worm as the name might imply. It is a fungus that sometimes grows in the shape of a ring.

RISK OF CONTRACTING: High.

TRANSMISSION: Contact with animals that have ringworm or with damp areas (like shower floors) where fungi grow.

PREVENTION:

☐ Keep skin folds clean and dry.

☐ Use powder after bathing.

☐ Don't pet cats or dogs that have ringworm.

☐ Avoid going barefoot on damp floors.

SYMPTOMS:

☐ Itchy, raised, reddish eruptions, sometimes in a ring shape.

☐ This ring of eruptions gradually enlarges.

☐ Ringworm of the scalp can produce round spots with scales and loss of hair.

TREATMENT:

☐ Wash the infected part daily with soap (preferably a disinfectant soap) and water, and dry well.

☐ Apply antifungal powder or cream (miconazole, clotrimazole, tolnaftate or others).

☐ Expose the infected part to the air and sunlight if possible.

☐ Wash all towels, underwear, and socks in hot water, and change them often.

■ SCABIES

RISK OF CONTRACTING: Moderate.

TRANSMISSION: Caused by a mite that burrows under the skin. It is spread by touching an infected person or through clothing or bedding. Also passed during sexual contact.

PREVENTION: Take great care with personal cleanliness.

SYMPTOMS:

☐ Very itchy bumps that can appear all over the body. They are most common between the fingers, on the wrists, around the waist, and on the genitals.

☐ To the naked eye, the burrows of the mites look like dirty ridges or streaks.

□ Itching is usually most severe at night. Scratching can cause infected sores, and sometimes swollen lymph nodes or fever.

TREATMENT:

□ Try not to scratch! Scratching the sores can lead to a bacterial infection.

□ Trim fingernails short so that live eggs can't get trapped under them if you scratch.

□ Bathe and change clothes daily.

□ Use lindane cream or lotion (*Kwell* or *Gamene*). Apply lindane over your entire body (except face) and leave for 12-24 hours before washing. During treatment, reapply to hands each time you wash them. A second application a week later may be required. It will take a few weeks for the itch and symptoms to disappear, but be patient; if the medication is used correctly, it should work.

□ *Do not* use lindane on infants, young children, or pregnant women. For these individuals, get medical advice on an alternate medication.

□ Boil all clothes, bed linens, and towels.

□ If the condition persists, get medical advice.

□ If one person in a household has scabies, everyone should be treated.

□ After treatment, itching may persist. Treat with *Benadryl* or similar medication.

■ LICE

There are three kinds of lice: head lice, body lice, and crab lice (found in the pubic area).

RISK OF CONTRACTING: Moderate.

TRANSMISSION: Lice are crawling insects and are spread through close contact with an infected person or the sharing of combs, towels, clothing, etc. Crab lice are usually transmitted during sexual intimacy.

PREVENTION: Take great care with personal cleanliness.

SYMPTOMS:
- ☐ Itching.
- ☐ Sometimes skin infections and swollen lymph nodes.

TREATMENT:
   BODY LICE:
- ☐ 1% malathion powder, 1% lindane powder, or *Kwell* cream.
- ☐ Wash all clothes and bedding in hot water.
- ☐ Bathe often.

   HEAD AND CRAB (PUBIC) LICE:
- ☐ *A-200 Pyrinate* shampoo or *Kwell* shampoo or lotion.
- ☐ To get rid of nits (lice eggs) remaining after treatment, comb hair with a fine-toothed comb.
- ☐ Use only freshly washed clothes and bedding.

■ BOILS

A boil (or abscess) is an infection with pus that forms under the skin. Sometimes it is caused by a puncture wound or an injection given with a dirty needle. A boil is painful and the skin surrounding it becomes red and hot. It can cause swollen lymph nodes and fever.

TREATMENT:
- ☐ Apply warm compresses several times a day.
- ☐ Let the boil break open by itself. After it opens, keep applying warm compresses. Allow pus to drain, but never squeeze the boil, since this could cause the infection to spread.
- ☐ If the boil causes swollen lymph nodes or fever, take penicillin, 1 250-mg tablet, 4 times a day for 5-7 days.

EYES

■ CONJUNCTIVITIS ("PINK EYE")

Conjunctivitis can be due to infections (viral or bacterial) or allergies.

INFECTIOUS CONJUNCTIVITIS

This infection is usually very contagious. If you have infectious conjunctivitis you should wash your hands after touching your eyes and be sure not to share towels with other people.

RISK OF CONTRACTING: Moderate.

PREVENTION: Plenty of sleep and a daily multivitamin supplement help prevent this infection.

SYMPTOMS:

- ☐ Redness, pus, swelling of eyes.

- ☐ Burning or itching sensation.

- ☐ Eyelids often stick together after sleep.

TREATMENT:

- ☐ Clean pus from the eyes with a clean cloth moistened with boiled water.

- ☐ Apply antibiotic eye ointment inside the lower eyelid. Do not take medications with chloramphenicol unless under care of an eye specialist.

- ☐ Be sure the infection gets cleared up; if not treated, it can lead to more serious complications and optical damage.

ALLERGIC CONJUNCTIVITIS

Allergic conjunctivitis is due to an allergic reaction to pollen or other airborne substances.

SYMPTOMS:

- ☐ Itching, redness, and watering of both eyes.

- □ No pus.

- □ Usually sneezing and itching of nose and ears.

TREATMENT:
- □ Oral antihistamines such as *Actifed, Drixoral,* or *Dimetapp.*

- □ For severe symptoms, ophthalmic solution drops may help.

■ **STIES**

This is a bacterial infection of the eyelid caused by rubbing the eye with dirty hands, or sometimes by gnats or flies alighting on the eyelid.

RISK OF CONTRACTING: Moderate.

PREVENTION: Observe the rules of hygiene (see pp. 23-27).

SYMPTOMS:
- □ A red, swollen lump on the eyelid, usually near its edge.

TREATMENT:
- □ Apply warm, moist compresses with a little salt in the water.

- □ Using an antibiotic eye ointment 3 times a day helps to clear it up and prevent more sties.

FEVERS AND PARASITIC DISEASES

Diseases caused by viruses and parasites are difficult to distinguish without medical help. Many of these diseases have fever as a primary symptom. Use the following descriptions to help you identify the possible cause of your illness.

■ **TYPHOID**

Typhoid is an infection of the stomach and intestines that affects the whole body. Immunization against typhoid gives only partial immunity.

RISK OF CONTRACTING: Low-moderate.

TRANSMISSION: Fecal-oral

PREVENTION: Typhoid vaccination (see p. 7). Observe the rules of hygiene.

SYMPTOMS:

FIRST WEEK:
- [ ] Begins like a cold or flu.

- [ ] Headache and sore throat.

- [ ] Fever rises a little more each day until it reaches 104°F (40°C) or more.

- [ ] Pulse is often slow for the amount of fever present. Take your pulse and temperature every half hour. If your pulse gets slower when the fever goes up, you probably have typhoid.

- [ ] Sometimes there is vomiting, diarrhea, or constipation.

SECOND WEEK:
- [ ] High fever, relatively slow pulse.

- [ ] A few pink spots may appear on the body.

- [ ] Trembling.

- [ ] Delirium.

- [ ] Weakness, weight loss, dehydration.

THIRD WEEK:
- [ ] If there are no complications, the fever and other symptoms slowly subside but the infection may continue.

TREATMENT:
- [ ] Get medical help.

- [ ] Hospitalization may be required.

□ Typhoid is usually treated with chloramphenicol, ampicillin, or *Bactrim*. (Do not take chloramphenicol without medical supervision.)

□ Lower the fever using cool, wet cloths.

□ Drink plenty of liquids—soups, juices, etc.—to avoid dehydration; eat nutritious foods, in liquid form if necessary; and stay in bed until the fever is completely gone.

■ TYPHUS

Typhus—a disease similar to typhoid—most often occurs in cool, highland areas.

RISK OF CONTRACTING: Extremely low.

TRANSMISSION: Bites from lice, rat fleas, mites, ticks.

PREVENTION:

□ Keep clean; get rid of lice.

□ Use insecticide or repellent in areas with ticks.

SYMPTOMS:

□ Begins like a bad cold.

□ After a week or more, fever sets in with chills, headache, cough, and pain in the muscles and chest.

□ A few days after the fever begins, a rash appears, first in the armpits and then on the main body, but not on the face, hands, or soles of the feet. The rash looks like many tiny bruises.

□ Fever lasts 2 weeks or more.

□ May be a cough during the first week of fever; this sometimes develops into lung inflammation.

□ In typhus spread by ticks and mites, there is often a large painful sore at the point of the bite, and nearby lymph nodes are swollen and painful.

TREATMENT:

☐ Get medical attention.

☐ Treatment usually consists of tetracycline, 2 250-mg capsules 4 times a day for 7 days.

■ MALARIA

Malaria is caused by a para-
site (one of four types of
Plasmodium) carried by the
Anopheles mosquito.

When a person is bitten by an infected mosquito, malaria parasites are injected into the bloodstream; they are then carried to the liver, where they multiply.

After days, weeks, even years, parasites are released from the liver back into the bloodstream. Here they go through a repeated cycle: they enter blood cells, mature, reproduce, then burst out again into the plasma.

Symptoms occur only when the malaria parasites are free in the blood plasma (every 48-72 hours) and vary by the type of *Plasmodium*.

Some types of malaria parasites can remain in the liver, to be released into the bloodstream months or even years later and cause a relapse (see pp. 172-173).

Malaria must be taken seriously because it can be fatal if not properly treated. Malaria is frequently misdiagnosed because the symptoms of the disease are similar to those of so many others.

RISK OF CONTRACTING: Moderate.

TRANSMISSION: Bite of an infected mosquito.

PREVENTION:

☐ Avoid mosquito bites. For a full discussion, see p. 27.

☐ Use antimalarial pills—see pp. 9-13.

SYMPTOMS:

☐ Begins with chills and often a headache. The chills may last 15 minutes to an hour.

☐ Chills are followed by fever, often 104°F (40°C) or more. During the fever stage, which lasts several hours, you are flushed, weak, and sometimes delirious. You may have headache, nausea, or diarrhea.

☐ Finally, you begin to sweat, and the fever goes down. Usually malaria attacks come every 2 or 3 days, but in the beginning there may be daily fever. Anyone who suffers from unexplained fevers should have their blood checked for malaria.

TREATMENT:

☐ Get medical attention immediately. With proper treatment, recovery is usually prompt.

☐ Usual treatment consists of 1,000 mg of chloroquine (600 mg base) all at once. Then 6 hours later, 500 mg chloroquine (300 mg base). Then 500 mg chloroquine (300 mg base) daily for 2 days.

☐ In chloroquine-resistant areas **if not using mefloquine for prevention:** *Fandisar,* 3 tablets in a single dose plus quinine sulfate, 650 mg, 3 times a day for 3-7 days. (See p. 12 for warnings on *Fandisar.*) Alternately, quinine sulfate, 650 mg 3 times a day for 3 days; **plus either** doxycycline, 150 mg twice a day for 7 days; **or** tetracycline, 250 mg 4 times a day for 7 days.

☐ Self-treatment with mefloquine is not recommended because of the frequency of serious side effects (e.g., hallucinations, convulsions) associated with high doses.

■ **YELLOW FEVER**

(Only in East, Central, and West Africa, Central America, and northern South America, see map p. 176)

This is one of the few diseases for which certain countries require proof of immunization. Yellow fever is particularly dangerous due to a relatively high fatality rate and lack of an effective medical treatment.

RISK OF CONTRACTING: Low.

TRANSMISSION: Bite of an infected mosquito.

PREVENTION:
- ☐ Immunization. All persons going to areas where there is yellow fever should get immunized prior to departure. (Immunization is good for 10 years.)
- ☐ Take precautions against mosquito bites (see p. 27).

SYMPTOMS:
- ☐ Severe headache, vomiting, nausea, muscle pain, and fever, 102° to 104°F (39° to 40°C), all occurring suddenly, often in the morning.
- ☐ Pulse rate rises for a few days to 100-110 beats per minute, then falls rapidly to about 50 beats per minute.
- ☐ In severe cases, there may be bleeding in the gastrointestinal tract and jaundice (characterized by yellowness of the skin and eyes).

TREATMENT:
- ☐ Obtain medical consultation.
- ☐ There is no specific medical treatment for yellow fever.
- ☐ Care consists of treating the symptoms of the disease by preventing dehydration (see pp. 49-50) and reducing fever (see p. 52).
- ☐ Bed rest and nursing care are important.

■ DENGUE FEVER

RISK OF CONTRACTING: Low.

TRANSMISSION: Bite of an infected mosquito.

PREVENTION:
- ☐ Take precautions against mosquito bites (see p. 27).
- ☐ No vaccine is available.

SYMPTOMS:

FIRST STAGE:

□ Chills, headache, muscle and joint aches, fever, often beginning suddenly.

□ Fever may go as high as 104°F (40°C).

□ Usually temporary flushing or pale pink rash, especially on the face.

□ Swollen lymph nodes.

□ After 48-96 hours, the fever goes down quickly, followed by profuse sweating. For about 24 hours there is no fever and you feel much better.

SECOND STAGE:

□ Fever returns, but usually doesn't go as high as the first time.

□ Usually a second rash appears, all over the body except the face. Palms of the hands and soles of the feet may be red and swollen.

□ If often takes several weeks to get over the weakness from this fever. An attack produces immunity for a year or more.

TREATMENT:

□ Get medical help.

□ Stay in bed and treat the fever as described on p. 52 and take the rehydration drink described on p. 50.

□ For headache and other aches, take acetaminophen (*Tylenol*), or if necessary, codeine, 15-60 mg every 4 hours. Do not take aspirin.

■ **JAPANESE ENCEPHALITIS**

The Japanese encephalitis virus produces no symptoms in most people that it infects. However, when symptoms do occur, the disease can be fatal. Transmission is most likely during the summer months in temperate areas and during the rainy season and early dry season in tropical areas when the mosquito populations are highest. Many of the symptoms of Japanese encephalitis are similar to other viral infections transmitted by the bite of mosquitoes.

RISK OF CONTRACTING: Low.

TRANSMISSION: Bite of an infected mosquito.

PREVENTION:

☐ Japanese encephalitis vaccine (see p. 8).

☐ Take precautions against mosquito bites (see p. 27).

SYMPTOMS:

☐ Headache, fever, chills, often beginning suddenly.

☐ Weakness, delirium, vomiting.

☐ Strong aversion to bright light.

☐ Stiff neck, sore muscles and joints.

☐ In advanced stages, convulsions, paralysis, coma.

TREATMENT:

☐ Get medical attention.

☐ In the meantime, prevent dehydration (see pp. 49-50) and if convulsions or shock should develop, treat as described on pp. 144-146.

■ MENINGOCOCCAL MENINGITIS

(Endemic to Sub-Saharan Africa, Tanzania, and Kenya; epidemics occur worldwide, most recently in Nepal and New Delhi, India. See map, p. 177)

Meningococcal meningitis can occur in epidemics and is most common in schoolchildren and in populations living under crowded conditions. **The onset of this disease is rapid and immediate diagnosis and treatment is essential.**

RISK OF CONTRACTING: Low-moderate in epidemic areas (if unvaccinated).

TRANSMISSION: Inhalation of infectious air droplets from people coughing and sneezing.

PREVENTION:

☐ Immunization if heading to an epidemic area (see p. 8).

☐ If you are exposed to the disease, the antibiotic rifampicin may offer protection. Adult dose is 600 mg for 3 days. **Caution:** Women on the Pill should use other forms of birth control because rifampicin can decrease the Pill's effectiveness. Another side effect of rifampicin is that it turns urine a dark brown.

☐ Avoid contact with known carriers.

SYMPTOMS:

☐ Sudden onset of chills, fever, severe headache, nausea and vomiting, stiff neck, general aches and pains.

☐ May be a rash of pinhead-sized spots.

☐ Mental confusion, convulsions, and coma may follow.

☐ Definitive diagnosis is determined by a lumbar puncture (spinal tap).

☐ Often fatal if not treated quickly.

TREATMENT:

☐ **Get medical help fast—every minute counts!**

☐ Treatment usually consists of penicillin injections or, if possible, penicillin given intravenously.

■ PLAGUE

(Most prevalent in Southeast Asia and Africa.)

Plague is a bacterial infection that occurs primarily in wild rodents (e.g., rats, mice, squirrels), but can be transmitted to humans through the bite of fleas. This disease is highly infectious and can be deadly.

RISK OF CONTRACTING: Very low.

TRANSMISSION: Bite of an infected rat flea.

PREVENTION:
- ☐ Avoid contact with rodents.
- ☐ Use repellents to minimize fleabites.
- ☐ Immunization (see p. 9) if you are heading to an epidemic area or if you anticipate contact with rodents.

SYMPTOMS:
- ☐ Sudden onset of repeated chills and fever rising to 103° to 106°F (39.4° to 41°C).
- ☐ Swollen lymph nodes and red, turning to black and blue, splotches under the skin.
- ☐ Mental confusion and shock.
- ☐ If untreated, coma and death may result.

TREATMENT:
- ☐ Obtain medical attention.
- ☐ Treatment with streptomycin or tetracycline and complete bed rest are required.

■ FILARIASIS

Filariasis is a disease of the blood and lymph caused by a worm transmitted by mosquito bites. Repeated infections over a number of years can cause enlargement of parts of the body, called elephantiasis.

RISK OF CONTRACTING: Low.

TRANSMISSION: Bite of an infected mosquito.

PREVENTION: Take precautions against mosquito bites (see p. 27).

SYMPTOMS:
- ☐ Symptoms begin 3-12 months after being bitten.

☐ Fever.

☐ Swelling and redness of lymph glands, but only after many years with the disease.

☐ May be headache, skin rash.

☐ The attack usually subsides after several days but may recur.

TREATMENT:

☐ Get medical attention.

☐ Usually treated with diethylcarbamazine, but only under medical supervision.

■ LEPTOSPIROSIS

RISK OF CONTRACTING: Low.

TRANSMISSION: Leptospirosis is carried by animals like dogs and rats, which pass the *Leptospira* organism in their urine. Direct contact with a diseased animal or with contaminated water can infect you.

PREVENTION:

☐ Avoid swimming, wading, or washing in water that may be contaminated.

☐ Avoid contact with infected animals.

SYMPTOMS:

☐ First stage: Headache, severe muscle aches, chills, and fever that begin suddenly. Four to 9 days with recurring chills and fever that often goes higher than 102°F (39°C). Then the fever goes down.

☐ Second stage: On the 6th through 12th day of illness, the fever and other symptoms recur.

☐ Sometimes in severe cases there is jaundice (yellowing of the skin and eyes that indicates liver involvement), anemia, hemorrhaging, or disturbances of consciousness.

TREATMENT:
- ☐ Get medical help.

RESPIRATORY INFECTIONS

■ COLDS AND FLU

Colds and the flu are caused by viruses and therefore cannot be cured with antibiotics or other medicines. There are drugs that can alleviate symptoms. Take care of colds early.

RISK OF CONTRACTING: High.

TRANSMISSION: Cold viruses float in the air and are breathed in. Colds do not come from being cold or wet.

PREVENTION:
- ☐ Get enough sleep and eat well.
- ☐ Eating vitamin-C rich foods and taking vitamin C supplements may help.

TREATMENT:
- ☐ Drink plenty of liquids and get enough rest.
- ☐ Take aspirin or *Tylenol* to reduce the fever and muscular aches that accompany colds and flu.
- ☐ *Do not* use antibiotics.

■ BRONCHITIS

Bronchitis is an inflammation of the bronchial tubes (air tubes between the throat and lungs). Bronchitis is usually caused by an allergy, infection (viral or bacterial), or irritation. It often follows a bout of influenza, measles, or whooping cough. Air pollution and smoking are contributing factors. The chief danger of untreated bronchitis is that it can lead to pneumonia.

RISK OF CONTRACTING: Low-moderate.

PREVENTION:

- [ ] Get plenty of rest, fresh air, and good food. Take care of colds and flu in their early stages.

- [ ] Avoid allergy-provoking substances such as dust, animals, and pollen.

- [ ] Avoid breathing polluted air and cigarette smoke.

SYMPTOMS:

- [ ] Cough, sometimes dry and hacking.

- [ ] Sputum: yellow-green if cause is bacterial; clear if viral.

- [ ] Chest congestion.

- [ ] Fever.

- [ ] Wheezing.

TREATMENT:

- [ ] Get medical attention.

- [ ] Bacterial bronchitis responds to antibiotics, usually: erythromycin, 250 mg, 4 times a day for 10 days; ampicillin, 500 mg 4 times a day for 10 days; or (if erythromycin is unavailable or you are allergic to penicillin), tetracycline, 500 mg 4 times a day for 10 days.

- [ ] Viral bronchitis: antibiotics do not help.

- [ ] Breathing hot vapors helps to loosen mucus and ease the cough. Glyceryl guaiacolate (*Robitussin*) helps to dissolve the phlegm in the bronchi.

- [ ] You can drain the bronchi through a process called "postural drainage." Breathe hot vapors or take a dose of *Robitussin* and then drink a glass of water to loosen mucus. Then lie on a bed (face down) with your head near the floor. Cough and move your head from side to side to alleviate symptoms.

- [ ] Drink plenty of water (12-20 cups) each day to replace lost fluids.

□ Humidify your room at night by boiling water or using a vaporizer if you have one.

■ PNEUMONIA

Pneumonia is an acute (sudden) infection of the lungs, which often occurs as a complication of other respiratory illnesses such as flu, bronchitis, asthma, or any very serious illness, especially in babies and old people.

RISK OF CONTRACTING: Low.

PREVENTION: Treat colds, bronchitis, or flu properly with plenty of fluids, good food, and rest, so pneumonia won't develop.

SYMPTOMS:
□ Rapid, shallow breathing, sometimes with wheezing.

□ Cough, often with yellow, greenish, or slightly bloody mucus.

□ May be chest pain and fever.

TREATMENT:
□ Get medical attention.

□ Take aspirin or *Tylenol* to lower fever and lessen pain.

□ Drink plenty of liquids.

□ Ease the cough and loosen mucus by drinking lots of liquids and breathing hot water vapors.

□ If medical care is not available, treatments, in order of preference, are:

   • erythromycin (250 mg 4 times a day for 7-10 days), **or**

   • ampicillin (500 mg 4 times a day for 7-10 days)—not for those allergic to penicillin, **or**

   • tetracycline (500 mg 4 times a day for 7-10 days).

■ "STREP" THROAT

A throat infection by beta hemolytic streptococcus bacteria is a common cause of a sore throat, especially in children and young adults.

RISK OF CONTRACTING: Low-moderate.

PREVENTION: General health maintenance (see pp. 28-37).

SYMPTOMS:
- ☐ Sore throat.
- ☐ Fever.
- ☐ Soreness and swelling of lymph nodes in the neck.
- ☐ Bad breath.
- ☐ "White" pustular spots (exudates) on the tonsils and back of throat.

TREATMENT:
- ☐ Get a throat culture, if available, to establish a definitive diagnosis since viral infections (which don't respond to antibiotics) may cause similar symptoms.
- ☐ Aspirin, throat lozenges, and warm saltwater gargles help relieve pain.
- ☐ Generally, if a sore throat lasts more than 3 or 4 days and is accompanied by high fever, and medical care is not available, one should consider antibiotics. Penicillin 500 mg 4 times a day for 10 days **or**, if you are allergic to penicillin, erythromycin 500 mg, 4 times a day for 10 days are usual.

HEPATITIS

Hepatitis is a disease of the liver, which can be caused by a number of different viruses. Note that the A and B forms of the virus are transmitted in very different manners.

■ HEPATITIS A (INFECTIOUS HEPATITIS)

Hepatitis A is common in areas where there are rudimentary sanitation facilities. Infected human waste enters the water system and is then spread to its many users. Hepatitis A is especially serious for pregnant women.

RISK OF CONTRACTING: Moderate.

TRANSMISSION: Fecal-oral. The disease is spread from person to person through improper hygiene or contaminated food and water, often by infected food handlers who don't wash their hands. It can also be transmitted during sexual intimacy.

PREVENTION:
- ☐ Get a dose of immune serum globulin (gamma globulin) before you go and a **booster dose every 4-6 months** while you are in an area of possible exposure (see p. 7).

- ☐ If you think you have been exposed to someone who has hepatitis A within the last 3 weeks, but you have no symptoms yet, a shot of immune globulin (IG) may protect you from the disease. **Do not** get IG if you already have symptoms of the disease.

- ☐ Avoid contaminated food and water.

SYMPTOMS:
- ☐ Headache, fever, nausea, vomiting, loss of appetite.

- ☐ Within 1-11 days there may be dark-colored urine, light- or clay-colored stools, and sometimes a yellowish tint to skin and/or eyes (indicates liver involvement).

□ Sometimes there is pain on the right side of the body near the liver.

□ In general, one is very sick for 2 weeks and remains very weak for 1-3 months afterwards.

□ Children up to approximately 12 years old can have hepatitis A without any signs of illness, but they can spread the disease.

TREATMENT:

□ It is important to get medical attention immediately if you think you have hepatitis A.

□ Antibiotics do not work against hepatitis A; some drugs will increase damage to the liver. **Do not use drugs.**

□ The only treatment is rest and drinking lots of liquids. If food is unappealing, try fruit or fruit juices. Taking vitamins may help increase your appetite.

□ Your needs for protein and energy are increased by this disease. When your appetite returns, increase your calorie intake by eating frequent small meals. Avoid fatty foods—they place added stress on the liver. **Do not drink alcohol** for a long time (more than 3 months) after being sick.

□ If you have hepatitis A, avoid passing the disease on to others: keep very clean, use a separate plate for eating, avoid sex (even with a condom), and do not handle food.

■ HEPATITIS B (SERUM HEPATITIS)

Hepatitis B is transmitted in a very different manner and is a more serious disease than hepatitis A. Health workers (who regularly handle blood and body fluids), homosexuals, and drug addicts are at particular risk.

RISK OF CONTRACTING: Low (see map, p. 174).

TRANSMISSION: Direct exchange of body fluids such as blood or semen of an infected person. Common pathways of transmission include sexual contact, the sharing of personal items (razors or combs), and unsterile hypodermic needles. There is a good chance a female carrier of hepatitis B will pass the virus to her child during birth. If you are pregnant and think you may have been exposed to the hepatitis B virus, you should be tested at a health facility to determine if you are a carrier.

PREVENTION:

- ☐ Hepatitis B vaccination (see pp. 8-9). The duration of protection and need for booster doses have not yet been determined. However, it appears that individuals who have developed antibodies following the 3 vaccine doses are protected for approximately 4 years.

- ☐ Choose sexual partners carefully (condoms are NOT absolute protection against hepatitis A or B).

- ☐ Avoid contact with blood, body fluids, and secretions of potential carriers.

- ☐ Avoid sharing personal hygiene items.

SYMPTOMS:

- ☐ Symptoms of hepatitis B are similar to those of hepatitis A, yet develop more slowly (clinical signs appear approximately 60-120 days after exposure). Symptoms can become very severe.

- ☐ Chronic fatigue, loss of appetite.

- ☐ In more severe cases, jaundice (yellowish tint to skin and/or eyes) and exhaustion.

- ☐ Fever is usually absent or mild.

- ☐ In a small percentage of individuals, the disease may cause permanent liver damage or liver cancer.

TREATMENT:

- ☐ Currently, there is no known treatment for chronic hepatitis B. Neither dietary restrictions nor drugs seem to be effective at altering the natural course of the disease.

□ If you believe you were exposed to the hepatitis B virus, you should get medical help as soon as possible; post-exposure treatment with hyperimmune globulin may help prevent the symptoms of the disease.

■ NON-A, NON-B HEPATITIS

There are at least two types of non-A non-B hepatitis. One type (now called hepatitis E) is like hepatitis A in terms of prevention, transmission, symptoms, and treatment, and has been reported in South Asia (southern Commonwealth of Independent States, Pakistan, Indian subcontinent, Burma, Indonesia), North Africa, and rural areas of Central Mexico. Travelers to these areas should receive immune globulin (IG) though the value of this against hepatitis E is still unknown. Prevention by following the rules of food and water hygiene is the best recommendation.

URINARY TRACT AND GENITALS

There are many different disorders of the urinary tract and genitals, some of which are difficult to tell apart. The ailments described below are those that are not necessarily transmitted sexually. Sexually transmitted diseases are discussed below (see pp. 102-115). Disorders of the urinary tract and genitals that are not sexually transmitted are almost exclusively confined to women.

The normal acid/alkaline (pH) balance in a healthy woman's vagina kills yeasts, fungi, and other harmful organisms. If the balance is upset, some organisms may multiply disproportionately, causing irritation to the tissues. The result may be abnormal discharge, itching and burning of the vulva, chafing of the thighs, and the need to urinate frequently. **Yeast infection** and **bacterial vaginosis** are two vaginal infections discussed below.

The likelihood of infection is often increased by lowered resistance, use of antibiotics, douching, sexual activity, pregnancy, use of birth-control pills, diabetes, or cuts, abrasions, or other irritations in the vagina.

■ PREVENTION OF URINARY TRACT AND GENITAL INFECTIONS:

FOR WOMEN:

- ☐ Don't go for long periods of time without urinating (i.e., drink plenty of fluids on a regular basis).

- ☐ Always wipe from front to back after a bowel movement or urinating.

- ☐ Keep the genital area clean and dry.

- ☐ **Do not** douche on a regular basis, since this may push bacteria into the uterus.

- ☐ Urinate before and after sexual contact.

- ☐ Avoid caffeine and alcohol, which irritate the bladder.

- ☐ Don't wear tight pants or synthetic underwear (cotton is best).

FOR MEN:

- ☐ Avoid sexual contact with a woman who has a urinary tract or genital infection.

- ☐ If you do have sex, use a condom and avoid oral sex.

■ WHILE TREATING URINARY TRACT AND GENITAL INFECTIONS:

FOR WOMEN:

- ☐ Abstain from sexual activity—it can irritate already fragile tissues.

- ☐ Sexual partners should also be treated for vaginal infections, even if they do not show symptoms.

☐ Avoid scratching—it irritates tissue and causes infection to spread.

☐ Keep the vulva clean and dry. Avoid tight pants.

☐ Don't stop the treatment as soon as the symptoms disappear; it often takes longer (7-10 days total) to completely cure vaginal infections.

FOR MEN:

☐ Seek medical treatment if your sexual partner has a vaginal infection.

■ BLADDER INFECTION

RISK OF CONTRACTING: Moderate.

TRANSMISSION: Bladder inflammation in women is usually caused by intestinal bacteria getting into the urinary tract. It is often triggered by sexual activity. Traveling is also conducive to bladder infections since sitting for long periods of time and the inability to bathe as often as usual can be enough to bring on a bladder infection. Bladder inflammation is more likely to occur during a period of lowered resistance (having another infection or disease, lack of sleep, poor diet, etc.).

PREVENTION: See p. 96 for a discussion of preventive measures.

SYMPTOMS:

☐ Frequent burning or painful urination; it sometimes feels as though the bladder does not empty.

☐ May be blood or pus in the urine. Urine may smell bad or look cloudy.

☐ Fever, nausea, and diarrhea may be present.

☐ Sometimes pain in the lower belly.

Note: Similar symptoms, combined with fever and pain in the side or middle back, indicate a kidney infection and require medical attention.

TREATMENT:

☐ **Drink a lot of water.** At least 1 glass every 30 minutes. Many minor urinary infections can be cured by simply drinking a lot of water, without the need for medicine.

☐ In addition to water, drinking large amounts (more than 3 quarts) of unsweetened cranberry, grapefruit, or orange juice every day can make your urine pH more acidic which inhibits the growth of bacteria.

☐ If the symptoms persist after drinking liquids, medication is usually prescribed. **Note:** The particular medication will depend on the type of bacteria causing the infection. It is best to get a urine "culture and sensitivity test" done to find out which type of bacteria is present.

☐ When symptoms have been present for under 48 hours, **or** you are *not* someone who gets bladder infections often (more than 3 a year), one of the following may be prescribed:

- Sulfasoxazole (*Gantrisin*) 2 grams (2,000 mg) all at once.

- Trimethoprim/sulfamethoxazole (*Septra, Bactrim*) 2 double-strength tablets all at once.

- Ampicillin (for persons allergic to sulfa-based drugs) 3.5 grams (3,500 mg) all at once.

- tetracycline (for persons allergic to ampicillin/penicillin) 500 mg 4 times daily by mouth for 10 days.

☐ If symptoms have been present for longer than 48 hours **or** you frequently get bladder infections (more than 3 in a year), one of the following may be prescribed:

- Trimethoprim/sulfamethoxazole (*Septra, Bactrim*), 1 double-strength tablet 2 times daily for 7-10 days.

- Sulfasoxazole 500 mg 4 times daily for 10 days.

- Ampicillin (for persons allergic to sulfa-based drugs) 500 mg 4 times daily for 10 days.

Note: Women taking antibiotics such as ampicillin or tetracycline often get a secondary yeast infection. To help prevent or treat this, while you are taking the antibiotic, follow the recommendations on pp. 99-100.

☐ For additional precautions while treating this infection, see pp. 96-97.

TO RELIEVE THE SYMPTOMS WHILE TAKING MEDICATION:

☐ Continue to drink a lot of water.

☐ Get plenty of sleep.

☐ Avoid caffeine and alcohol, which irritate the bladder.

■ YEAST INFECTION (CANDIDIASIS)

RISK OF CONTRACTING: moderate

PREVENTION: See p. 96 for a discussion of preventive measures.

SYMPTOMS:

☐ Thick white discharge that may look like cottage cheese and smell like mold, mildew, or baking bread.

☐ Severe itching, usually most severe right before menstruation.

☐ Lips of the vulva may be red and sore.

☐ Burning urination.

TREATMENT:

☐ At first signs, douche with yogurt or milk that contains live culture but no sugar or honey.

☐ If infection persists, get medical care. Medical treatment usually consists of nystatin (*Mycostatin*), miconazole (*Monistat*) or clotrimazole (*Mycelex*), as vaginal suppositories or cream, for 3-7 days. (Women who are in their first 3 months of pregnancy should not receive miconazole.)

☐ Avoid sexual intercourse. If you do have sex, medications should be used following, not prior, to intercourse.

□ For additional precautions while treating this infection, see pp. 96-97.

Warning: Never use antibiotics against this kind of infection; they only make yeast infections worse.

■ BACTERIAL VAGINOSIS (GARDNERELLA, HAEMOPHILUS)

RISK OF CONTRACTING: Low-moderate.

PREVENTION: See p. 96 for a discussion of preventive measures.

SYMPTOMS:

□ Thin, white or clear, non-irritating discharge that may smell "fishy."

TREATMENT:

□ This discharge is common and often clears in a few days without treatment.

□ If it doesn't clear in 2 weeks, try douching with one of the following douches:

- Vinegar douche: (2 tablespoons vinegar in 1 quart water) used twice daily for 10-14 days.

- *Betadine* douche: (2 tablespoons *Betadine* in 1 quart warm water) once daily for 10-14 days.

- Hydrogen peroxide douche: (1 part HP 3% to 2 parts water) twice daily for 3 days, then once daily for 4 days. **Note:** Do not make more than one douche at a time, as hydrogen peroxide becomes inactive when it sits in water for awhile.

□ If none of the douches works, an effective medicine is metronidazole (*Flagyl*) 500 mg taken by mouth 2 times daily for 7 days. Outside the U.S., *Flagyl* is often given as vaginal suppositories; these are just as effective as the oral drug. **Caution:** *Do not* drink alcohol when taking metronidazole, as this causes severe nausea. Do not use *Flagyl* if you are pregnant.

□ If pregnant, or *Flagyl* doesn't work, clindamycin 300 mg by mouth 2 times a day for 7 days.

□ For additional precautions while treating this infection, see pp. 96-97.

■ TRICHOMONIASIS ("TRICH")

RISK OF CONTRACTING: Low-moderate.

TRANSMISSION: This infection is most often contracted through sexual intercourse, though it can also be spread by towels, underwear, or other moist objects.

PREVENTION: See p. 96 for a discussion of preventive measures.

SYMPTOMS:

IN WOMEN:

□ Itching, usually just after menstruation.

□ Thin, foamy, yellow-green or gray, foul-smelling vaginal discharge.

□ Burning urination.

□ Genitals may be swollen and sore.

IN MEN:

□ Usually none, occasionally a mild discharge from the penis.

TREATMENT:

□ Treatment usually consists of oral doses of metronidazole (*Flagyl*) either 2 gms (2,000 mg) all at once **or** 250 mg 3 times daily for 7 days. You may experience some side effects (e.g. headache, nausea) while taking metronidazole. **Caution:** *Do not* drink alcohol when taking metronidazole, as this causes severe nausea. *DO NOT* take if pregnant.

□ Alternate treatment: clotrimazole (*Mycelex* tablets or cream) vaginally each night prior to bed for 7 days.

□ Although males usually do not have symptoms, they should be treated if their female partner is experiencing symptoms.

□ For additional precautions while treating this infection, see pp. 96-97.

SEXUALLY TRANSMITTED DISEASES (STDs)

Sexually transmitted diseases (STDs) have become extremely common. In Asia, Africa, and Latin America, as elsewhere, there is a chance of getting one of the STDs if you are sexually active and do not take proper precautions. Having one of these diseases in a developing country can be emotionally and physically trying because it is often difficult to obtain understanding and qualified medical care. Follow the recommended precautions described below to avoid catching STDs, but if you notice any symptoms which may indicate an STD, get medical attention immediately. Most STDs are quite easy to cure if caught early, but can have serious consequences if not promptly and properly treated.

Though a description of the usual medical treatment is included under each disease, you should *not* take any medications unless you have consulted a doctor and are sure of which STD you have.

■ TO PREVENT CATCHING OR SPREADING SEXUALLY TRANSMITTED DISEASES:

THE ONLY FOOLPROOF WAYS TO AVOID GETTING STDs ARE:
☐ Not having sexual contact.

☐ Having sexual contact with just one partner who does not have any of the STDs.

IF YOU CHOOSE TO BE SEXUALLY ACTIVE WITH A NUMBER OF DIFFERENT PARTNERS:
☐ Choose sexual partners carefully.

☐ Wash genitals before and after sexual contact.

☐ Urinate after sexual activity to help flush away bacteria (especially important for women).

☐ Condoms offer the best mechanical barrier to the transmission of STDs. Diaphragms, contraceptive creams, jellies, or foam all offer some protection. But, the best protection if you are sexually active is a condom *and* a vaginal spermicide. **Note:** The Pill and the IUD may actually promote the growth of bacteria associated with STDs. You should use another form of contraception in addition to the Pill or the IUD as protection against STDs.

☐ If you have any symptoms that might be due to an STD, however mild, get medical attention at once.

■ IF YOU DETERMINE THAT YOU HAVE AN STD:

☐ Tell everyone with whom you have been sexually active, so they can also get treated. Because women often do not show any symptoms until the disease has already progressed, it is particularly important to tell a woman if you may have passed an STD on to her. Both men and women can unknowingly pass STDs on to others.

☐ While treating STDs, *do not* have sexual contact.

☐ To be effective, medication must be taken as directed and for the full length of time (see pp. 42-45).

☐ After taking the complete medication regimen, get retested to be sure that the STD has been cured. You may have to repeat a medication or try a different drug to fully eliminate the STD.

☐ Women: Since it is more difficult for you to tell if you have an STD (especially gonorrhea), you may wish to be routinely tested for these during general physical and gynecological exams.

☐ Women: Routine douching is not recommended (except to treat vaginal infections, see pp. 99-100).

Note: In addition to the sexually transmitted diseases discussed below, there are some diseases which can be, but are not necessarily, sexually transmitted. These are discussed in other sections of this book:

☐ Trichomoniasis (see p. 101)

☐ Hepatitis B (see p. 95)

☐ Crab (Pubic) Lice (see pp. 74-75)

■ GONORRHEA ("CLAP")

RISK OF CONTRACTING: Moderate.

PREVENTION: See pp. 102-103 for a discussion of preventive measures.

SYMPTOMS:

IN MEN:

☐ Burning pain or difficulty when urinating.

☐ Drops of pus from the penis. Discharge may be thin and clear or thick and creamy and can vary in color from yellowish to greenish.

If not treated, after weeks or months:

☐ Painful swelling in the knees, ankles, or wrists.

☐ Rash or sores all over the body.

☐ Fever.

☐ May get infections of the prostate, epididymitis.

☐ Sterility (can't have children).

IN WOMEN:

☐ At first, there are often **no symptoms.**

☐ There may be slight pain when urinating and/or during sex or slight vaginal discharge (thick and yellow).

If not treated after weeks or months:

☐ Pain in the lower abdomen (pelvic inflammatory disease, see pp. 108-109).

☐ Menstrual problems.

☐ High risk of sterility.

☐ Urinary problems.

In men, the first symptoms of gonorrhea may begin 2-5 days (or up to 3 weeks or more) after sexual contact with an infected person. In women, weeks may pass before any signs of the disease show up. Even though a woman shows no symptoms, she can give the disease to someone else. If a pregnant woman with gonorrhea is not treated before giving birth, the infection may harm her baby's eyes.

Since there are relatively few signs of gonorrhea (especially in women), it is a good idea to get tested regularly if you suspect exposure. A person (especially a woman) with a gonococcol infection will often have a chlamydial infection at the same time (see pp. 107-108).

TREATMENT:

☐ Get medical help.

☐ One of the following may be prescribed:

- Ampicillin (a type of penicillin) 3.5 grams (3,500 mg) by mouth all at once plus probenecid, 1 gram (1,000 mg) by mouth all at once. (Ampicillin will work without probenecid, but not as well.)

- Tetracycline (for those allergic to penicillin), 500 mg 4 times each day for 7 days.

- Doxycycline (for those allergic to penicillin), 100 mg 2 times each day for 7 days.

- Ceftriaxone (*Rocephan*) 250 mg, intramuscular injection (IM) **and** doxycycline or tetracycline as above.

- Ciprofloxacin, 500 mg orally as a single dose, particularly in penicillin-resistant areas (parts of Southeast Asia, West Africa).

Since people with gonorrhea often have a chlamydial infection also, some doctors will treat both at once (see pp. 107-108 for the treatment of chlamydia).

Note: There is a strain of gonorrhea, penicillinase-producing

Neisseria gonorrhoeae (PPNG), which is resistant to penicillin. It has been found that PPNG can, however, be cured with other medications such as spectinomycin.

■ NONGONOCOCCAL URETHRITIS (NGU)
NONGONOCOCCAL VAGINITIS (NGV)

In both men and women, some infections have symptoms similar to gonorrhea but are not caused by it. These infections are called nongonococcal infections. A common nongonococcal infection **in men**, is referred to as NGU and may be caused by various microorganisms, including chlamydia (see discussion, on pp. 107-108) or ureaplasma. **In women**, these same organisms can cause infections of the tissues of the reproductive organs (uterus, fallopian tubes, ovaries); these infections are referred to as NGV. The symptoms of NGU and NGV are usually milder and take longer to appear than those caused by gonorrhea.

In both men and women, it is common to have both gonococcal and nongonococcal infections at the same time. Therefore, it is recommended by the CDC that both infections be treated together (see pp. 104-106 for treatment of gonorrhea).

RISK OF CONTRACTING: Low-moderate.

PREVENTION: See pp. 102-103 for a discussion of preventive measures.

SYMPTOMS:

IN MEN:

☐ Painful urination and discharge.

☐ Burning and itching around the opening of the penis.

☐ Other symptoms are similar to those of gonorrhea, but milder.

IN WOMEN:

☐ As with gonorrhea, there are few symptoms of NGV in women. However, abnormalities of the cervix associated with NGV would show up in a Pap smear.

TREATMENT:

☐ Obtain medical attention.

☐ Determine, through clinical tests, whether your symptoms are due to gonorrhea or something else.

☐ Medication is usually one of the following:

- Tetracycline, 500 mg 4 times daily for 7 days.

- Doxycycline, 100 mg twice daily for 7 days.

- Erythromycin (for those who can't take tetracycline or doxycycline), 500 mg 4 times daily for 7 days.

- Ceftriaxone (*Rocephan*) 250 mg IM **and** doxycycline **or** tetracycline as above.

- Ciprofloxacin, 500 mg, orally as a single dose, particularly in penicillin-resistant areas (parts of Southeast Asia, West Africa).

Note: Untreated NGU or NGV can lead to epididymitis (in men), pelvic inflammatory disease (in women) and sterility (in both sexes). It is important, therefore, that sexual partners notify each other if NGU or NGV has been diagnosed so that the partner can be treated also.

Caution: Women taking antibiotics often get a secondary vaginal infection, usually yeast. To prevent this, see p. 99.

■ CHLAMYDIA

Chlamydia are sexually transmitted microorganisms that are responsible for certain nongonococcal infections in both men and women. Chlamydia can cause nongonococcal urethritis and vaginitis (see previous discussion) and may lead to pelvic inflammatory disease in women (see pp. 108-109). It is thought to be the leading cause of infertility everywhere, especially in women. Estimates by the CDC are that in the U.S., at least 45% of persons diagnosed with gonorrhea also have chlamydia. Therefore, they recommend that persons being treated for gonorrhea be treated for chlamydia at the same time.

RISK OF CONTRACTING: Moderate-high.

PREVENTION: See pp. 102-103 for a discussion of preventive measures.

SYMPTOMS:
- ☐ The symptoms of chlamydia are similar to those of gonorrhea, but much less severe. Therefore the condition is likely to go untreated.

- ☐ Symptoms are more likely in males.

TREATMENT:
- ☐ Treatment for chlamydia usually consists of one of the following:

  - Tetracycline, 500 mg by mouth, 4 times daily for 7 days.

  - Doxycycline, 100 mg by mouth, twice daily for 7 days.

  - Erythromycin (for persons allergic to tetracycline or doxycycline), 500 mg by mouth, 4 times daily for 7 days.

Note: Tetracycline and doxycycline will work for both gonorrhea and chlamydia. But ampicillin (penicillin) works only for gonorrhea.

- ☐ Chlamydia should be treated promptly to avoid further complications.

■ PELVIC INFLAMMATORY DISEASE (WOMEN ONLY)

Pelvic inflammatory disease (PID) is a term used to describe a severe infection of a women's reproductive organs (uterus, fallopian tubes, ovaries). PID is often caused by gonorrhea or chlamydia. Women who use IUDs are more likely to suffer from this disease.

RISK OF CONTRACTING: Low-moderate.

PREVENTION: See pp. 102-103 for a discussion of preventive measures.

SYMPTOMS:
- ☐ The most common symptom of PID is pain and tenderness in the pelvic region and lower back, especially during movement or sexual intercourse.

☐ Other symptoms vary according to the individual and the bacteria involved, and may include: increased menstrual cramps, pain, and bleeding; nausea, vomiting, and loss of appetite; vaginal discharge, burning during urination.

TREATMENT:

☐ Get medical attention (hospitalization may be required).

☐ Treatment usually involves cefoxitin (250 mg IM) plus doxycycline (100 mg orally, 2 times a day for 10 days) or tetracycline (500 mg orally, 2 times a day for 10 days). Do not take either of these if pregnant. (Since the bacterial cause of the PID is often difficult to determine, a combination of medications is common.)

☐ In addition to treating the infection with medication, a woman recovering from PID must allow the tissues to mend by resting, eating well, and avoiding intercourse.

■ SYPHILIS

RISK OF CONTRACTING: Low.

PREVENTION: See pp. 102-103 for a discussion of preventive measures.

SYMPTOMS:

☐ The first sign is usually a sore, called a **chancre**, which appears 2-10 weeks after sexual contact with a person who has syphilis. The chancre may look like a pimple, a blister, or an open sore. It usually appears on the genitals, or less commonly, on the lips, fingers, anus, or inside the mouth. This sore is full of infection, which is easily passed on to others. The chancre is usually painless. If it is inside the vagina, a woman may not know she has it, but she can still infect others.

☐ The sore lasts a few days to a few weeks and then disappears without treatment. **But the disease continues to spread** through the body.

☐ Weeks or months later, there may be sore throat, mild fever, mouth sores, or swollen joints. Or there may be a painful rash all over the body, ring-shaped welts, or an itchy rash on the hands and feet.

☐ All these symptoms usually go away by themselves—**but the disease continues.**

☐ Not treated, syphilis may, years later, cause heart disease, paralysis, insanity, and many other problems.

If any strange rash or skin condition appears days or weeks after a pimple or sore on the genitals, it may be syphilis. If any of the above symptoms occur, get medical advice.

TREATMENT:

☐ Get medical help.

☐ If caught early (less than one year after exposure), treatment usually consists of one of the following:

  • A penicillin injection (2.4 million units, IM)

  • Tetracycline **or** erythromycin (for persons allergic to penicillin), either one, 500 mg taken orally, 4 times each day for 15 days.

☐ Avoid sexual contact during treatment and for 1 week afterwards.

■ HERPES

Herpes viruses cause sores on the genitals, abdomen, and thighs (**genital herpes**) and on the lips, mouth, and face (**oral herpes**). Though annoying, this disease does not ordinarily lead to medical difficulty. So far, there is no cure for herpes.

RISK OF CONTRACTING: Low-moderate.

TRANSMISSION: Direct contact with herpes sores of an infected person. For oral herpes this usually means kissing, for genital herpes, sexual intimacy. Oral to genital sex can transmit the virus between mouth and genitals.

PREVENTION: See pp. 102-103 for a discussion of preventive measures.

SYMPTOMS:

☐ One or more painful, tiny fluid-filled blisters, which most commonly appear on the lips or on the genitals of both men and women. These usually develop 2-20 days after contact with the virus.

☐ These blisters burst and form open sores, which can last up to 2 weeks.

☐ These sores dry up and form a scab.

☐ In addition to the sores, there may be flu-like symptoms such as fever, aches, chills, and fatigue; the lymph nodes in the groin can be swollen and tender. These symptoms are most common during the first-time infection.

☐ Women may have trouble urinating.

The first time people get herpes, the symptoms are usually most severe. After the first episode, about half of these people never get the sores again, even though they still carry the virus. If the sores do come back, they ordinarily recur in the same place, but they do not last as long.

In women, genital herpes, especially the initial episode, can complicate pregnancy.

TREATMENT:

☐ There is no medicine that will cure herpes. There are medicines available to reduce the pain and symptoms.

☐ The drug *Acyclovir* is helpful in reducing symptoms. The oral form, 200 mg, 5 times a day for 10-14 days is preferable to the ointment, except during pregnancy. *Acyclovir* may be difficult to obtain overseas; take it with you if you will need it.

☐ If you are suffering from herpes, keep the area clean and dry. Avoid touching or scratching the sores. Be particularly careful of touching the sores and then rubbing your eyes. Wash your hands often.

- [ ] For genital herpes, avoid tight clothing that irritates the sores. Wear cotton underpants, which do not retain moisture.

- [ ] *Do not* have sexual contact while the blisters or sores are present.

- [ ] If you have suffered from herpes in the past, keep your genital area clean and watch for signs of recurrent infection.

- [ ] Pregnant women who have herpes must inform their health specialist of this. If a woman is having an outbreak at the time she is to give birth, some medical practitioners recommend a cesarean section to prevent infection in the baby.

Maintaining general good health (through good nutrition and plenty of rest) and avoiding stress will decrease the likelihood and severity of recurrent cases.

■ HIV INFECTION AND AIDS

AIDS (for Acquired Immunodeficiency Syndrome) is a disease that damages part of the body's immune system needed to fight off infections and diseases. AIDS is caused by the Human Immunodeficiency Virus, or HIV. A person can be infected with HIV and not develop the signs and symptoms of AIDS until many years after infection. However, anyone who has been infected is a "carrier" and may pass the virus on to others.

Without treatment, current estimates are that 75-100% of all HIV-infected people will develop AIDS within 10-15 years. During this time, these individuals may show milder symptoms, called "HIV disease" (formally called AIDS-related Complex or ARC).

Once a person is infected with HIV, the body is more susceptible to a wide variety of diseases that a healthy body would be able to ward off. It is these diseases, not the AIDS virus itself, that result in death. Though the majority of AIDS sufferers in the U.S. have been homosexual men and intravenous-drug users, proportionally more people are becoming infected with HIV through heterosexual contact. In some regions (e.g., Central Africa and Haiti), heterosexual transmission is common.

RISK OF CONTRACTING: Low for individuals who take the precautions outlined below; moderate-high for intravenous drug users and sexually active individuals who do not practice safe sex.

TRANSMISSION: Direct exchange of body fluids such as blood, semen, and vaginal secretions. The virus cannot pass through healthy skin, but does pass through the mucous membranes of the vagina, rectum, and possibly, mouth. These are common pathways of transmission:

☐ Vaginal or anal sexual intercourse with an infected person. Transmission during oral-genital sex is rare, except during menstruation.

☐ Sharing hypodermic needles with an infected person.

☐ Blood transfusions if the donated blood is infected with HIV. A blood-screening process to detect the AIDS virus is now widely used in the industrialized countries, but *do not* count on this in less-developed countries.

☐ Perinatally: an infected woman can pass the virus to her baby during pregnancy or, possibly, while breast-feeding.

There is *no* evidence that HIV can be transmitted by:

☐ Casual contact such as shaking hands or embracing.

☐ Using public facilities such as bathrooms, phones, water fountains, etc.

☐ Bites of insects such as mosquitoes or ticks.

PREVENTION:

☐ There is currently no vaccine against HIV.

☐ Use the same precautions recommended in preventing other sexually transmitted diseases (see pp. 102-103).

☐ Avoid sexual contact with high-risk individuals including prostitutes (of either sex), intravenous-drug users, sexually active individuals, and hemophiliacs.

☐ Do not allow semen, blood, or vaginal secretions of an infected individual to enter your body.

☐ Use latex condoms for all types of sexual intercourse. Animal-skin condoms have pores that allow HIV to pass. Do not store condoms in the sunlight.

☐ The spermicide, nonoxynol 9, in contraceptive foams, jellies, and creams, helps to inactivate the virus. Preparations should contain at least 5% nonoxynol 9; **use in addition to a condom**.

☐ Do not share hypodermic needles, razors, or toothbrushes.

☐ If you receive injections, make sure the needle is sterile. This is also true for acupuncture needles and needles used for ear piercing, tattooing, and dental procedures.

☐ Avoid locally produced blood products and immune globulins (IG, see p. 7) unless you are confident they are safe.

☐ Medical personnel working with HIV infected individuals are at risk of "needle-sticks" and other routes of transmission and should follow the infection-control procedures recommended by the CDC.

SYMPTOMS:

☐ HIV disease and AIDS lead to a wide range of signs and symptoms; listing them here is impractical.

☐ Know your HIV status by getting a confidential HIV test.

TREATMENT:

☐ Currently, there is no cure for HIV infection or AIDS.

☐ A number of drugs are presently being used to control HIV and prevent death from AIDS. To date, the effectiveness of these drugs is unclear.

☐ **Important:** If you test positive for HIV, you should get expert medical attention immediately.

IF YOU HAVE HIV OR AIDS:

☐ Over 50 countries restrict the entrance or travel of HIV-infected people. If you are infected, contact the embassy of the foreign country you are planning to visit to get the latest information.

☐ Vaccinations are generally safe for individuals with HIV or AIDS. The exceptions are yellow fever, oral polio (OPV), oral typhoid, and plague vaccines.

MISCELLANEOUS

■ TETANUS

Tetanus is a deadly disease—be sure your immunization is up to date.

RISK OF CONTRACTING: Moderate (if unvaccinated).

TRANSMISSION: The tetanus microorganisms live in human or animal feces and enter the body through a wound. These type of wounds can easily cause tetanus: gunshot and knife wounds and puncture wounds from thorns, nails, splinters, or barbed wire.

PREVENTION:

☐ Immunization against tetanus (see p. 7).

☐ Avoid puncture wounds.

TREATMENT:

☐ Any time you have a wound, clean it well and protect it. If the wound is big, deep, or dirty, get medical attention. You may need a tetanus booster shot.

■ RABIES

RISK OF CONTRACTING: Low.

TRANSMISSION: Rabies comes from the bite of an animal infected with rabies, or from the saliva of an infected animal that gets into a wound or scratch. Animals that spread rabies include dogs, cats, foxes, wolves, racoons, jackals, bats, and cattle. A rabid animal acts strangely (restless or irritable), foams at the mouth, and cannot eat or drink. It may go mad and bite anyone nearby. The animal usually dies within 5-7 days.

PREVENTION: Avoid any animal that seems sick or acts strangely.

TREATMENT:

If you have any reason to believe that a rabid animal has bitten someone:

☐ Tie or cage the animal for a week.

☐ Immediately clean the bite well with soap, water, and hydrogen peroxide. Do not close the wound.

☐ If the animal dies before the week is up, or if it was killed or cannot be caught, get medical help at once.

The first symptoms of rabies appear 10 days to 2 years after the bite (usually within 3-7 weeks). Treatment must begin **before** the first signs of illness appear. Once the disease begins, no medical treatment known can save the person's life.

■ SCHISTOSOMIASIS (BLOOD FLUKES)

(Most prevalent in tropical Africa and Brazil, also, areas of Asia, northern South America and the Caribbean, see map, p. 177.)

Schistosomiasis is caused by a worm (blood fluke) that gets into the bloodstream. It is spread when an infected person defecates into water. Worm eggs in the feces hatch and live inside a certain kind of small water snail. The worms then leave the snail host and penetrate the skin of a person who has contact with contaminated water.

RISK OF CONTRACTING: Moderate.

TRANSMISSION: Swimming, wading, washing in, or drinking contaminated water.

PREVENTION:

☐ If you are in an area where schistosomiasis exists, avoid all contact with water that could be contaminated. (There is no risk in sea-water.)

- ☐ If you accidentally come into contact with contaminated water, dry off immediately with a towel (and apply alcohol, if available). It takes the worms several minutes to penetrate the skin.

- ☐ In endemic areas, all bathing and washing water should be boiled or chlorinated. Or store water in a snail-free container for 2-3 days before using it.

SYMPTOMS:

- ☐ At first, skin irritation and rash where worm larvae penetrated the skin; this rash disappears after a day or two.

- ☐ Then, for 4-6 weeks there are no symptoms while the worms mature.

- ☐ Subsequent to this period, symptoms are fever, chills, weakness, and a rash on the body.

- ☐ Painful and bloody urination and diarrhea are common.

- ☐ Also, enlargement of the liver and spleen, swelling of the lymph nodes, and pain in the back, groin, and legs may occur.

- ☐ In advanced cases (after months or years), there may be abdominal swelling, liver problems, and damage to the central nervous system potentially resulting in death.

TREATMENT:

- ☐ Get medical care.

- ☐ Treatment with a new drug, praziquantel (*Biltricide*), has been encouraging, but strict preventive measures should still be followed since the disease can do irreversible damage before infection is detected.

■ LIVER FLUKES (CLONORCHIASIS, OPISTHORCHIASIS)

(Found in East and Southeast Asia.)

Liver flukes (worms) are transmitted when an animal or human that is already infected defecates in freshwater (not saltwater) streams and rivers. The worms are then eaten by snails, which then pass young worms into the flesh of fish. Humans get infected by eating fish containing the worms.

RISK OF CONTRACTING: Low.

TRANSMISSION: Eating raw fish that is infected. Salted, pickled, smoked, dried, or partially cooked fish may still be infected.

PREVENTION: Make sure that the fish you eat is well cooked or free from infection.

SYMPTOMS:

☐ Often there are no symptoms.

☐ Symptoms include: tiredness, low-grade fever, an enlarged and tender liver, pain in the "pit" of the stomach, and worms and worm eggs in feces.

TREATMENT:

☐ Get medical attention.

☐ The best medication is praziquantel (*Biltricide*), 25 mg per kg (2.2 lbs) body weight, 3 times a day, after meals for 2 days. Or mebendazole (*Vermox*) 100 mg 2 times each day for 3 days. Or *Bithromol*, 30-50 mg per kg of body weight every other day for 10-15 days.

☐ Chloroquine is *not* recommended.

■ SLEEPING SICKNESS (AFRICAN TRYPANOSOMIASIS)

(Found in Africa between 15°N and 20°S latitude.)

The characteristic sleepiness of this disease occurs only in its final stages; note preliminary signs and treat the disease early.

RISK OF CONTRACTING: Low.

TRANSMISSION: Bite of the tsetse fly.

PREVENTION:

- [ ] Take precautions against insect bites (see p. 27).

- [ ] The drug pentamidine has been used to prevent the disease; however, it is not generally recommended since it is potentially toxic and may obscure the symptoms of the disease in its early, more easily treated, stages.

SYMPTOMS:

- [ ] A small chancre (sore) at site of a tsetse fly bite develops a few days after being bitten.

- [ ] The sore then gets painful and hard at the center with a swollen area of 3-4 inches (7-9 cm) in diameter surrounding it.

- [ ] High fever, headache, rash, enlarged lymph nodes, apathy, painful swellings, and an inability to concentrate typically occur 10 to 21 days later.

- [ ] Untreated, the disease may affect the central nervous system (this can take weeks or years depending on the type of infection).

- [ ] In its final stages, the most common symptoms are laziness and sleepiness. Later, coma and death may result.

TREATMENT:

- [ ] Get medical attention immediately.

- [ ] Medical treatment is successful if started when the disease is in its early stages.

■ CHAGAS' DISEASE (AMERICAN TRYPANOSOMIASIS)

(Found in Mexico and South and Central America.)

This disease usually affects children and young adults in rural areas. Mud and cane houses provide the breeding places for the reduviid bug. The reduviid bug bites at night.

RISK OF CONTRACTING: Low.

TRANSMISSION: Bite an an "assassin" or "kissing" reduviid bug. The reduviid bug is a brown, oval bug about an inch long.

PREVENTION: Take precautions against insect bites (see p. 27), especially at night.

SYMPTOMS:

☐ A painless, purplish swelling, usually on the eye, mouth, or face.

☐ Fever and enlargement of the lymph nodes occur after 1 or 2 weeks. There may be diarrhea and vomiting.

☐ The body is usually able to eliminate the disease on its own and symptoms will disappear.

☐ Sometimes, however, the disease will remain and, untreated, can lead to serious damage of the heart and internal organs months, years, or even decades later.

TREATMENT:

☐ If you think you have been bitten by an infected reduviid bug, you should get medical tests to make sure that the infection has been eliminated.

☐ Certain medicines can treat Chagas' disease in its early stages, but once later symptoms appear, there is no cure.

■ RIVER BLINDNESS (ONCHOCERCIASIS)

(Found in West, Central and East Africa, southern Mexico, Central America, northern South America.)

This disease is caused by tiny worms that are carried from person to person by small, humpbacked flies or gnats known as blackflies (simulids).

These flies breed in fast-moving water. Thus, the disease is more prevalent in areas with an abundance of streams.

RISK OF CONTRACTING: Low.

TRANSMISSION: A bite of an infected fly or gnat. Flies usually bite during daylight hours.

PREVENTION: Protect against fly bites with proper clothing. Repellents may help (see p. 27).

SYMPTOMS:
- [ ] There may be severe rash and itching and skin can become thick, dark, and scaly.

- [ ] After many years, eye problems often develop. First redness and tears, then corneal scarring, and finally, blindness.

- [ ] Sometimes, several months after a blackfly bites and passes the worms into the body, **lumps** begin to form under the skin. (In the Americas, these lumps are on the head and upper body; in Africa, on the lower body and thighs.)

- [ ] The lumps slowly grow to a diameter of about an inch (2-3 cm). Often, there are no more than 3-6 lumps; these are usually painless.

TREATMENT:
- [ ] Get medical attention.

■ LEISHMANIASIS

A group of related protozoan infections that affect either the internal organs (Kala Azar) or the skin.

RISK OF CONTRACTING: Low.

TRANSMISSION: The bite of sandflies.

PREVENTION: Prevent sandfly bites with repellents and proper clothing (see p. 27).

SYMPTOMS:

KALA AZAR:

☐ Fever, followed by the enlargement of the spleen, liver, and other internal organs.

SKIN LEISHMANIASIS:

☐ Single or multiple nonhealing sores, 1/4-1 inch (1-2 cm) in size, on the face, arms, and legs.

☐ A form found in Central America and northern South America is characterized by similar sores that affect the nose and mouth.

TREATMENT:

☐ Get medical attention.

■ ANTHRAX

(Most prevalent in Haiti, Africa, the Middle East, and Asia.)

Goatskin handicrafts from Haiti have been found to be infected with anthrax and thus are not allowed into the United States.

RISK OF CONTRACTING: Low.

TRANSMISSION: Contact with infected animals and their products (e.g., goatskin drums, wool products, and animal hides). The spores that cause infection may persist on a contaminated item and remain infectious for many years.

PREVENTION:

☐ Avoid contact with infected animals and their products.

☐ A vaccine is available for those at high risk (e.g., veterinarians).

SYMPTOMS:

☐ An expanding open sore with a red rim and dark (blue or black) center.

☐ May be headache, nausea and/or vomiting.

TREATMENT:

☐ Obtain medical attention.

☐ Antibiotics are the usual medical treatment.

■ BRUCELLOSIS (UNDULANT FEVER, MALTA FEVER)

This disease is caused by microorganisms passed from animals to people.

RISK OF CONTRACTING: Low.

TRANSMISSION: Drinking fresh milk from infected cows or goats. Microorganisms can enter through scrapes or wounds of persons who work with sick cattle, goats, or pigs. Infection can also occur by breathing microorganisms into the lungs.

PREVENTION:

☐ Drink only cow's or goat's milk that has been boiled or pasteurized.

☐ In areas where brucellosis is a problem, avoid cheese that has been made with unboiled milk.

☐ *Do not* handle infected cattle, goats, and pigs. Be careful if you have any cuts or scrapes.

SYMPTOMS:

☐ Starts gradually with increasing fatigue, loss of appetite, headache, stomachache, and general aches and pains.

☐ Irregular (rising and falling) fever and chills appear after a few days. Drenching sweats follow.

☐ Fevers may be mild or severe. Fever usually begins with afternoon chills, rises to 104° or 105°F (40° or 41°C) and ends with sweating in the early morning.

☐ May be swollen lymph nodes.

☐ Untreated, the symptoms will subside, but the disease is still present and symptoms may recur.

TREATMENT:

☐ Get medical attention. Treatment is long and expensive.

☐ Treatment usually consists of tetracycline, 2 250-mg capsules 4 times a day for 21 days.

Heat, Cold, And High Altitude

Some ailments are caused by extreme environmental conditions. This chapter discusses health concerns in very hot and very cold climates as well as at high altitude. Most of these ailments have warning signs; be aware of early signals and take protective measures *before* the situation becomes serious.

HEALTH PROBLEMS CAUSED BY HEAT

■ HEAT CRAMPS

Heat cramps occur in hot weather to people who sweat a lot. They occur because of a lack of salt.

RISK OF CONTRACTING: Moderate.

PREVENTION:

☐ Make sure that you get enough salt in your diet.

☐ Protect against dehydration (see pp. 49-50) and take precautions when exercising in the heat (see pp. 35-36).

SYMPTOMS:

☐ Cramps in the legs, arms, or stomach.

☐ There may be vomiting.

TREATMENT:

☐ Put a teaspoon of salt in a quart (4 cups or 1 liter) of water and drink it. Repeat every hour until the cramps are gone.

☐ Sit or lie down in a cool, shady place and gently massage the painful areas.

☐ Stretching the affected muscle will often help.

■ HEAT EXHAUSTION

Heat exhaustion usually occurs in people who sweat a lot in hot, humid weather.

RISK OF CONTRACTING: Low-moderate.

SYMPTOMS:

☐ Person is very pale and weak and perhaps feels faint.

☐ The skin is cool and clammy.

☐ The pulse is rapid and weak. (Normal pulse: 60-80 beats per minute in an adult.)

☐ Headache

☐ Body temperature is normal or below normal.

☐ Vomiting is common.

☐ Person is *not* necessarily thirsty.

TREATMENT:

☐ Lie down in a cool, shady place and remove excess clothing.

☐ Raise your feet above your head, and rub your legs.

☐ Drink saltwater: 1 teaspoon of salt in a quart (liter) of water. Drink 3-5 quarts (12-20 cups) in 12 hours. (Do not force an unconscious person to take liquids.)

☐ Recovery is usually rapid, but take it easy and use extra salt for the next few days.

■ HEATSTROKE (SUNSTROKE)

Heatstroke is not common but is very dangerous. It occurs in hot weather, especially in older people, chronic alcoholics, diabetics, and persons with poor circulation.

RISK OF CONTRACTING: Low.

SYMPTOMS:
- ☐ The skin is red, dry, and very hot. Not even the armpits are moist.
- ☐ The person has a very high fever, sometimes more than 108°F (42°C) and the pulse pounds.
- ☐ Unconsciousness is common.

TREATMENT:
- ☐ **The body temperature must be lowered immediately.**
- ☐ Put the person in the shade and remove excess clothing.
- ☐ Soak the victim with cold water (ice water if possible). If a tub is available, the person should be immersed in cold water.
- ☐ Fan the victim.
- ☐ Continue the treatment until the fever drops to below 102°F (39°C) then cover with blanket or dry clothing to prevent chilling.
- ☐ Seek medical help as soon as possible.

DIFFERENCES BETWEEN 'HEAT EXHAUSTION' AND 'HEATSTROKE'

HEAT EXHAUSTION
- sweaty, pale, cool skin
- large pupils
- no fever
- weakness

HEATSTROKE
- red, dry, hot skin
- high fever
- the person is very ill or unconscious

HEALTH PROBLEMS CAUSED BY COLD

In cold environments, the presence of wind increases the body's rate of evaporation and heat loss. Take extra precautions if these conditions exist.

■ CHILBLAINS

Chilblains occur in damp, cold climates. Chilblains frequently affect people who live in accommodations that are not well heated.

PREVENTION:
- ☐ Keep your extremities dry and warm.
- ☐ Wear rubber gloves when washing dishes or clothes
- ☐ Wash your feet in warm water and dry them well before you go to bed.
- ☐ If the room that you sleep in is poorly heated, use hot water bottles in bed.
- ☐ Exercise to improve your circulation.

SYMPTOMS:
- ☐ Itchy, painful swellings that can lead to open sores on the face, hands, and/or feet.

TREATMENT:
- ☐ Do not irritate chilblains by rubbing them or continuing to expose them to dampness and cold.
- ☐ Keep chilblains dry and warm.
- ☐ Apply hydrocortisone cream.

■ FROSTBITE

Frostbit is the freezing of skin and tissues. It happens to someone who is not dressed warmly enough in extremely cold conditions. Frostbite usually occurs on the hands and feet, but sometimes on the face and ears. **It is very dangerous.** If completely frozen, the skin will die and later turn black. The affected body part may have to be amputated.

PREVENTION:

- ☐ Dress properly (using layers of loose clothing) and make sure you have enough extra clothes for unexpected weather or emergencies (e.g., falling into a cold stream).

- ☐ Carry extra gloves, plenty of warm (wool) socks and a hat that covers your ears.

- ☐ Eat lots of carbohydrates and fats as heat sources.

- ☐ Avoid smoking and consuming alcohol or caffeine in cold weather.

- ☐ Be attentive to the first indications of frostbite. Take time to warm yourself before severe frostbite sets in.

SYMPTOMS:

- ☐ At first, there is cold, numbness, or pain in an extremity of the body.

- ☐ Then all feeling is lost as the part gets more frozen.

- ☐ The part gets pale in color and feels hard to the touch.

Note: If the person's skin still feels soft when touched, it is probably just a mild form of frostbite.

TREATMENT OF MILD FROSTBITE:

- ☐ Wrap the part with dry cloth and slowly rewarm it against another area of your body (or someone else's). Armpits or between the thighs are good places to warm hands or feet.

- ☐ Blowing on a mildly frostbitten part with warm breath may be enough.

TREATMENT OF SEVERE FROSTBITE:

Caution: Do not start treatment for severe frostbite until you are in a place where the person's whole body can be kept warm during and after treatment. It is better to let a hand or foot stay frozen for several hours than to let it get warm and then freeze again. If you must walk, do so on frostbitten feet until you get to a suitable location.

AS SOON AS SEVERE FROSTBITE IS DIAGNOSED:

☐ Start heading towards or preparing a warm shelter while protecting the frostbitten part from additional freezing.

☐ Remove rings and loosen clothing that may be inhibiting circulation.

☐ *Do not* try to warm the part by rubbing it with snow, hands, or cloth.

ONCE WARM SHELTER AND ADEQUATE FACILITIES ARE AVAILABLE:

☐ Fill a large container with warm (*not* hot) water that feels comfortable when you hold your hand in it. The temperature of the water should be between 102°F to 108°F (38.9°C to 42.2°C). If you have one, use a thermometer to verify this range since tissue damage can result if the part is re-warmed at temperatures either higher or lower than this.

☐ Remove all clothing from the frozen part.

☐ Soak the frozen part in the water until the part gets warm.

☐ If the water cools, add more warm water. But take out the person's hand or foot while you do this. Because the person cannot feel the temperature of the water, there is a danger of burning the part.

☐ As it gets warm, the frozen part will become painful. Give aspirin or codeine.

☐ When the part is no longer frozen, the person must stay warm and rest.

☐ Elevate the part and do not allow clothes or blankets to irritate or put pressure on it.

☐ Obtain medical help as quickly as possible since infection is common.

■ LOSS OF BODY HEAT (HYPOTHERMIA)

Hypothermia occurs when a person's internal body temperature is below normal. It usually happens on cold, wet, windy days to people who are tired, poorly clothed, and hungry. **It is very dangerous.** Often, a person does not realize what is happening. Mental confusion often accompanies hypothermia and may cause the person not to seek help. Extreme hypothermia can lead to death in just hours.

PREVENTION:

☐ Wear proper clothing. You can lose up to 50% of your body heat through your head and hands, so wear a hat and mittens to prevent these losses.

☐ Eat high-energy foods frequently and drink plenty of fluids.

☐ Be cautious of heavy physical exercise in cold environments. It can lead to heat loss, depletion of body fluids, and fatigue—all contributing factors to hypothermia. Stay warm, but avoid heavy sweating, which will evaporate and overly cool the skin and body.

☐ In bad weather, find protection from the wind and the elements.

SYMPTOMS:

☐ At first, uncontrolled shivering and pallor (pale skin).

☐ Then, confusion and dizziness.

☐ Movements are slow and clumsy; the person has difficulty walking.

☐ The person feels very tired.

☐ In advanced stages, breathing is shallow and pulse rate is slow.

☐ Can lead to loss of consciousness.

TREATMENT FOR MILD HYPOTHERMIA:

Warning: *Do not* heat up the person too fast as this can cause heart problems or even death.

- ☐ Quickly get the person to a dry place that is not windy.

- ☐ Replace wet clothing with warm, dry clothes.

- ☐ Make sure the head, feet, and hands are covered.

- ☐ Put the victim in a sleeping bag or under dry blankets.

- ☐ Have one or more people get in the sleeping bag also and hold the victim. Their body heat will warm the person who is hypothermic.

- ☐ Have the person drink warm, sugared liquids.

- ☐ Have the person eat sweet things like candy or ripe fruit. If you do not have sweets, give whatever food is available; starchy foods like bread and potatoes are good.

- ☐ *Do not* give alcohol.

- ☐ Encourage the victim to stay awake and move his or her legs and arms until body temperature returns to normal.

If the person stops shivering but still has any of the above signs, or is unconscious, the hypothermia is severe.

TREATMENT FOR SEVERE HYPOTHERMIA, INCLUDING UNCONSCIOUSNESS:

- ☐ Remove all of the victim's clothes and put victim in the warmest sleeping bag or blankets available. Pile other sleeping bags and clothes on top.

- ☐ Have two people remove their own clothes and get in the sleeping bag with the victim. Hold the victim tightly. Direct skin contact provides the most warmth.

- ☐ You can use rocks that have been warmed in a fire and wrapped in cloth, and hot water bottles as additional sources of warmth.

- ☐ *Do not* give an unconscious person food or drink.

- ☐ If the person does not regain consciousness, get medical help *fast.*

GENERAL CONCERNS
AT HIGH ALTITUDE

At high altitude, **cold weather, reduced oxygen, dry air, and intense sunlight** put unique strains on your body. Take precautions against these elements to avoid unnecessary illness or injury. Protect yourself with proper clothing, quality eye glasses, good nutrition, adequate fluid intake, and an awareness of proper rates of ascent.

In addition to the ailments discussed below, see the discussion of health concerns caused by cold (pp. 128-132) as cold weather often goes hand-in-hand with high altitude.

■ CLOTHING FOR THE MOUNTAINS

Wear **layers of clothes** to insulate warmth against your body. A number of thinner articles of clothing will allow you to regulate your body temperature as you exercise. It is as important not to get over-heated as it is to be warm enough. The fabric should be loosely woven to allow water vapor from your skin to escape. Polypropylene and wool are the best materials for under layers. Outer layers may need to be water and windproof. Gore-Tex is expensive, yet both repels water and breathes. Wear a loose woolen cap to prevent heat from escaping through your head.

■ DEHYDRATION

It is very easy to become dehydrated in the mountains. Your lungs exhale increased amounts of water because of the dry, oxygen-scarce air. Also, the strenuous hiking that is often part of mountain travel will cause you to lose extra water through sweat.

In order to prevent dehydration, it is important that you **drink lots of fluids** while in the mountains. Individual needs vary, but generally, you should drink **at least 12 cups (3 liters) per day**. At high altitude, the thirst mechanism is suppressed, so **you must push yourself to drink liquids, even if you don't feel thirsty.**

Remember, the best way to determine if you are getting enough liquid is by urine output. Small amounts of dark yellow urine indicate dehydration. The more you urinate, the lighter the urine is in color, the better. (See pp. 49-50 for additional information on dehydration.)

■ SUNBURN

(See pp. 52-53 for additional discussion)

At higher altitudes, more of the sun's ultraviolet rays penetrate the atmosphere. You must protect your skin against these rays by using ample amounts of **sunscreen or sunblock** on your face, ears, and nose (including the underside).

The best protection against sunburn is provided by physical barriers such as hats, scarves, and masks. Remember, even though it is not hot, you can still get severely burned.

■ SNOW BLINDNESS

Snow and ice reflect large amounts of the sun's rays. These rays can cause your eyes to water, burn, swell, and become intolerant to bright light. This syndrome is known as **snow blindness** and can be prevented by proper eye protection. Your sunglasses or goggles should be designed to protect against ultraviolet rays and have side-pieces. If you are walking on or near snow, wear glasses even during overcast conditions. Fortunately, snow blindness is temporary, and will reverse itself in a few days if you prevent additional exposure. During recovery, pain may be severe. Cold compresses and applications of an eye (opthalmic) ointment may help.

MOUNTAIN SICKNESS

High altitude (10,000 feet or 3,000 meters) and the decreased oxygen levels that accompany it, can cause a group of symptoms commonly referred to as **mountain sickness** or high altitude sickness. The various conditions associated with mountain sickness range in severity from mild to life-threatening and need to be taken seriously.

Acute mountain sickness is the term used to describe the most common symptoms occurring at high altitude and is characterized by headache, nausea, and sleeplessness. More serious ailments include increased fluid in the lungs (**pulmonary edema**) and swelling of the brain tissues (**cerebral edema**). To prevent all of these conditions, the rule to remember when climbing is **ascend slowly, and if you feel poorly or become ill, descend quickly**.

PREVENTION OF MOUNTAIN SICKNESS:

☐ Climb Slowly!

- As you head into the mountains, go to an intermediate altitude (6,000-8,000 feet or 2,000-2,500 meters) and rest for a few days before going higher.

- Avoid taking a mechanized vehicle (car, plane) to high altitudes. Above 10,000 feet (3,000 meters), walk up to let your body acclimatize better.

- Do not sleep at an elevation that is more than 1,000 feet (300 meters) higher than you slept the previous night. You can climb higher than this during the day, but then descend. It is the elevation at which you sleep that is important. A mountaineer's maxim is "**carry high and sleep low.**"

☐ Avoid dehydration.

☐ Do not overexert yourself—if you feel tired or short of breath, *rest!*

☐ Eat high-carbohydrate meals and snack on high-energy foods (peanuts, dried fruit, etc.).

□ Tobacco and alcohol should be avoided.

□ *Diamox* (acetazolamide) is a medication that may reduce the chance of acute mountain sickness. Dosage is 250 mg (1 tablet) 2-3 times a day for the first few days at high altitude. **Caution:** This is a powerful drug so you should consult a health professional before taking it, especially if you suffer from hypertension or heart problems.

■ ACUTE MOUNTAIN SICKNESS (AMS)

MILD AMS

PREVENTION: For prevention of AMS, see previous page.

SYMPTOMS:

□ Nausea and slight headache (which disappears after an aspirin or a night's sleep).

□ Difficulty sleeping and eating.

□ Shortness of breath.

These symptoms are often most apparent on the second or third day at high altitudes and are worse in the mornings.

TREATMENT:

□ These initial symptoms are a warning! You need more time to ac-climatize.

□ Spend an extra day and night without gaining altitude.

□ Follow the recommendations in the section entitled **Prevention of Mountain Sickness.**

□ Do light activity (e.g., walk, do chores around the camp) rather than napping, which tends to make symptoms worse.

MODERATE AND SEVERE AMS

SYMPTOMS:

□ Severe headache, weakness, breathlessness at rest, nausea, vomiting.

- ☐ Confusion, loss of coordination.

- ☐ Insomnia (inability to sleep).

- ☐ Reduced urine output.

TREATMENT:
- ☐ **Descend immediately!** A person suffering from moderate or severe AMS must descend 1,000-2,000 feet (300-600 meters).

- ☐ Drink fluids to avoid dehydration.

■ HIGH ALTITUDE PULMONARY EDEMA AND CEREBRAL EDEMA

These are the most dangerous forms of mountain sickness and may cause death if not recognized and treated promptly.

PREVENTION: For prevention of AMS, see pp. 135-136.

SYMPTOMS:
- ☐ Both have symptoms similar to severe acute mountain sickness.

- ☐ **High altitude pulmonary edema** is additionally characterized by a bad cough, excessive fatigue, "tightness of the chest," mental confusion, and ultimately unconsciousness and death.

- ☐ **Cerebral edema** is recognized by extreme confusion, memory loss, headaches, and dizziness.

TREATMENT:
- ☐ **Immediate descent** is required! Administer oxygen while descending, if available. Carry the victim if possible.

First Aid—
For Illness Or Injury

Familiarize yourself with these first-aid procedures, especially if you will be away from major cities and tourist routes. In many areas, there may not be an ambulance or hospital nearby. Knowing the basics of first aid could make an important difference in an emergency.

EMERGENCY FIRST AID

■ HOW TO CONTROL BLEEDING FROM A WOUND

□ Raise the injured part.

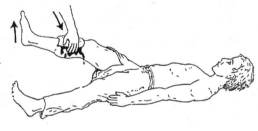

□ With a clean cloth (or your hand if there is no cloth) press directly on the wound.

□ Keep pressing until the bleeding stops. This may take 15 minutes or sometimes an hour or even more.

□ Don't remove the cloth if it gets red with blood—just add more cloth.

Caution: Tourniquets (a tightly tied cloth or band around the arm or leg that prevents blood flow) are extremely dangerous and should not be used except to control the flow of blood when an extremity has been completely cut off.

■ INTERNAL BLEEDING

SYMPTOMS:

- □ Coughing up or vomiting blood or "coffee ground" material; blood in the urine or feces; black stools.

TREATMENT:

- □ Have the person lie flat and breathe deeply.

- □ Get the person to a hospital or health center at once.

■ HEAD INJURIES

Bleeding from the scalp can be very heavy even when the injury is not so serious. If there is bleeding from the ear after an injury, it usually means there is a skull fracture.

TREATMENT:

- □ Be very careful not to apply too much pressure over the wound; this could cause bone chips from a possible fracture to be pressed into the wound.

- □ Don't bend the person's neck. It could be broken.

- □ Get medical help.

■ CHOKING

When food or something else sticks in someone's throat and the person cannot speak or breathe, *quickly* do the "Heimlich Maneuver":

- □ Stand behind the victim and wrap your arms around the waist.

- □ Put your fist against the belly above the navel and below the ribs.

☐ Press into the belly with a **sudden**, strong, upward jerk. This forces air out from the lungs and should clear the throat.

☐ Repeat several times if necessary.

If the person is a lot bigger than you, or is already unconscious, *quickly* do this:

☐ Lay the person face up.

☐ Tilt the head to one side.

☐ Sit over the person, put the heel of your lower hand on the person's belly between the navel and ribs.

☐ Make a quick, strong, upward push.

☐ Repeat several times if necessary. If the person still cannot breathe, try **mouth-to-mouth resuscitation** (see next page).

■ WHAT TO DO WHEN BREATHING STOPS: MOUTH-TO-MOUTH RESUSCITATION

COMMON CAUSES FOR BREATHING TO STOP ARE:

☐ Something stuck in the throat

☐ The tongue or thick mucus blocking the throat of an unconscious person

☐ Drowning, choking on smoke, or poisoning

A person who has stopped breathing will die unless breathing begins again soon. If a person stops breathing, begin mouth-to-mouth resuscitation *immediately*

DO ALL OF THE FOLLOWING AS QUICKLY AS YOU CAN:

☐ Remove anything stuck in the mouth or throat. Pull the tongue forward. If there is mucus in the throat, try to clear it out.

☐ Lay the person face up, tilt the head back, and pull the jaw forward.

☐ Pinch the nostrils closed with your fingers, open the mouth wide, cover the mouth with yours, and blow strongly into the lungs so that the chest rises. Lift your mouth away to let the air come back out and then blow again. Repeat about 15 times per minute (once every 4 seconds).

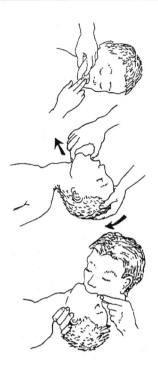

☐ Continue mouth-to-mouth resuscitation until the person can breathe without your assistance, or until there is no doubt that the person is dead. Sometimes you must continue mouth-to-mouth resuscitation for an hour or more.

■ **WHAT TO DO IF THE HEART HAS STOPPED BEATING: CARDIOPULMONARY RESUSCITATION (CPR)**

Cardiopulmonary resuscitation (CPR) is a way to revive someone whose heart has stopped beating. This technique uses a combination of mouth-to-mouth resuscitation and manual compression of the heart. Special training is necessary to learn CPR. Courses are available through hospitals and Red Cross chapters. It is recommended that everyone learn this lifesaving technique.

■ DROWNING

A person who has stopped breathing has only minutes to live! You must act fast!

Start mouth-to-mouth resuscitation at once (see previous page), if possible, even before the drowning person is out of the water.

Always start mouth-to-mouth resuscitation at once, before trying to get water out of the drowning person's chest.

If you cannot blow air into the person's lungs, when you reach the shore, quickly lay the person face up, with the head lower than the feet, and push the belly as described under "Choking" (see pp. 140-141). Then continue mouth-to-mouth resuscitation.

■ LOSS OF CONSCIOUSNESS

COMMON CAUSES OF LOSS OF CONSCIOUSNESS ARE:

☐ Drunkenness.

☐ A hit on the head (getting knocked out).

☐ Shock (see pp. 144-145).

☐ Poisoning (see pp. 146-147).

☐ Fainting (from fright, weakness, etc.).

☐ Heatstroke (see p. 127).

☐ Stroke.

☐ Heart attack.

IF A PERSON IS UNCONSCIOUS AND YOU DO NOT KNOW WHY, IMMEDIATELY CHECK EACH OF THE FOLLOWING:

Is the person:

☐ **breathing well?** If not, tilt the head back and pull the jaw and tongue forward. If something is stuck in the throat, pull it out. If the person is not breathing, use mouth-to-mouth resuscitation at once (see p. 141).

☐ **losing a lot of blood?** If so, control the bleeding (see p. 138).

☐ **in shock** (moist, pale skin; weak, rapid pulse)? If so, lay the person with the head lower than the feet and loosen clothing (see pp. 144-146).

☐ **suffering from heatstroke** (no sweat, high fever; hot, red skin)? If so, shade the person from the sun, keep the head higher than the feet, and soak the person with cold water (ice water if possible) (see pp. 127-128).

☐ **experiencing hypothermia** (in cold weather)? If so, begin re-warming (see pp. 131-132).

☐ **suffering from mountain sickness?** If so, immediately descend to a lower altitude and use oxygen if available (see pp. 135-137).

IF THERE IS ANY CHANCE THAT THE UNCONSCIOUS PERSON IS BADLY INJURED:

☐ It is best not to move the victim; wait until the person regains consciousness. If you have to move the person, do so with great care, because if the neck or back is broken, any change of position may cause greater injury.

☐ Look for wounds or broken bones, but move the person as little

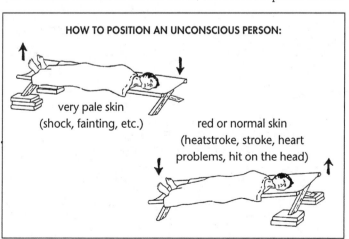

HOW TO POSITION AN UNCONSCIOUS PERSON:

very pale skin
(shock, fainting, etc.)

red or normal skin
(heatstroke, stroke, heart
problems, hit on the head)

as possible. Do not bend the back or neck.

☐ **Never give anything by mouth to a person who is unconscious.**

■ SHOCK

Shock is a life-threatening condition that develops when there is a severe reduction of blood to the tissues of the body. It can result from large burns, the loss of blood, severe illnesses, dehydration, or severe allergic reactions.

SYMPTOMS:

☐ Weak, rapid pulse (more than 100 beats per minute).

☐ "Cold sweat"; pale, cold, damp skin.

☐ Mental confusion, weakness, or loss of consciousness.

PREVENTION AND TREATMENT:

AT THE FIRST SIGN OF SHOCK OR IF THERE IS RISK OF SHOCK:

☐ Have the person lie down with the feet higher than the head, like this (unless there is a head or chest injury):

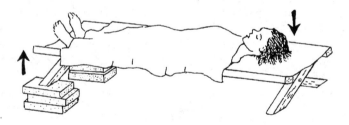

☐ Loosen clothing.

☐ If the person feels cold, cover with a light blanket.

☐ If the person is conscious, give plenty of fluids (but not alcohol).

☐ If the person is in pain, give aspirin or another pain medicine. Use codeine (not one with a sedative) for extreme pain.

☐ Keep calm and reassure the person.

IF THE PERSON IS UNCONSCIOUS:

☐ Lay the person on his or her side. The head should be low, tilted back and facing the ground. In case of choking, pull the person's tongue forward with your finger.

☐ If the person has vomited, clear the mouth immediately. Be sure the head is low, tilted back, and facing the ground so the victim does not breathe vomit into the lungs.

☐ Do not give the person anything by mouth until the person is fully conscious.

☐ If you or someone nearby knows how, give intravenous solution (normal saline) at a fast drip.

☐ Seek medical help fast.

■ ELECTRIC SHOCK

TREATMENT:

☐ Don't touch the person until you are sure that the electricity has been turned off. Shut off the power at the plug, circuit breaker, or fuse box.

☐ If the person is in contact with a wire or downed power line, use a dry stick to move it away.

☐ Check for breathing—if the person's breath is weak or has stopped, start mouth-to-mouth resuscitation immediately (see pp. 140-141).

☐ Get medical help. While you wait, keep the person warm. Give nothing to eat or drink until the person has been seen by a doctor or health worker.

■ SEIZURES (CONVULSIONS)

A seizure or convulsion is an uncontrolled, sudden jerking of all or part of a person's body, as in meningitis or epilepsy.

TREATMENT:

☐ Let the seizure run its course.

☐ Help the person lie down to avoid injury; keep the person from falling onto furniture or sharp objects; loosen clothing.

☐ Use no force; do not try to restrain the person.

☐ Afterward: check for breathing; give mouth-to-mouth resuscitation if necessary; check for burns around the mouth. This would indicate poison (see below).

☐ Stay with the person and make sure breathing continues. When the person seems able to move, get medical attention.

■ POISONING

SOME COMMON POISONS TO WATCH OUT FOR:

☐ Rat poison.

☐ DDT, lindane, sheep dip, and other insecticides.

☐ Medicine (any kind when too much is swallowed).

☐ Tincture of iodine.

☐ Bleach and detergents.

☐ Rubbing or wood alcohol.

☐ Poisonous leaves, seeds, or berries.

☐ Kerosene, gasoline, petrol.

☐ Lye.

TREATMENT:

If you suspect poisoning AND the victim is conscious, do this immediately:

☐ Make the person vomit. Vomiting can be induced by having the person put a finger down in the back of the throat, by giving the person a tablespoon of syrup of ipecac, or having the person drink water with soap or salt in it.

☐ Have the person drink as much as possible of milk, beaten eggs, or flour mixed with water. If you have it, give the victim a tablespoon of powdered charcoal mixed with water. These substances soak up some of the poison and thus can reduce its toxicity. Keep giving more milk, eggs, or flour and keep the person vomiting until the vomit is clear.

Caution: *Do not* make someone vomit who has swallowed kerosene, gasoline (petrol), or strong acids or corrosive substances (e.g., lye).

☐ If a person swallows one of these substances, neutralize the poison with milk, or if you don't have milk, give water or milk of magnesia.

☐ If the person feels cold, cover with a blanket, but avoid too much heat.

☐ **If poisoning is severe, get medical help immediately!**

■ EMERGENCY PROBLEMS OF THE GUT (ACUTE ABDOMEN)

Acute abdomen is a name given to a number of sudden, severe conditions of the gut for which prompt surgery is often needed to prevent death. Appendicitis, peritonitis, and gut obstruction are examples. Often the exact cause of acute abdomen will be uncertain until a surgeon operates.

In women, acute abdominal pain can also be caused by pelvic inflammatory disease or a pregnancy outside the uterus (ectopic pregnancy).

If a person has continuous severe gut pain with vomiting, but does not have diarrhea, suspect an acute abdomen.

SYMPTOMS:

ACUTE ABDOMEN: TAKE TO A HOSPITAL—SURGERY MAY BE NEEDED:

☐ Continuous severe pain that keeps getting worse.

☐ Constipation and vomiting.

☐ Belly swollen, hard, person protects it.

☐ Severely ill.

LESS SERIOUS ILLNESS: PROBABLY CAN BE TREATED AT A HEALTH CENTER:

☐ Pain that comes and goes (cramps).

☐ Moderate or severe diarrhea.

☐ Has had pains like this before.

☐ Only moderately ill.

■ APPENDICITIS, PERITONITIS

These dangerous conditions often require surgery. Seek medical help fast.

Appendicitis is an infection of the appendix. An infected appendix sometimes bursts open, causing peritonitis.

Peritonitis is an acute, serious infection of the lining of the cavity or bag that holds the gut. It results when the appendix or another part of the gut bursts open.

SYMPTOMS:

☐ The main sign is a steady pain in the belly that gets worse and worse.

☐ The pain often begins around the navel ("belly button"), but it soon moves to the lower right side.

☐ There may be a loss of appetite, vomiting, constipation, or a mild fever.

A TEST FOR APPENDICITIS OR PERITONITIS:

Slowly but forcefully, press on the abdomen a little above the left groin until it hurts a little.

Then quickly remove the hand.

If a very sharp pain (**rebound pain**) occurs when the hand is removed, appendicitis or peritonitis is likely.

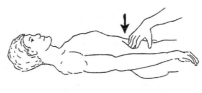

If no rebound pain occurs above the left groin, try the same test above the right groin.

OR:

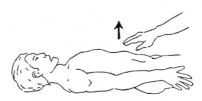

Have the person cough and see if this causes sharp pain in the belly. If it does, this is a sign of peritonitis.

TREATMENT:

☐ Seek medical help immediately. If possible, take the person to a place where surgery can be performed.

☐ **Do not give anything by mouth** and do not give an enema. Only if the person begins to show signs of dehydration, give sips of water or rehydration drink (see p. 50)—but nothing more.

☐ The person should rest very quietly in a half-sitting position.

Note: When peritonitis is advanced, the belly becomes hard like a board, and the person feels great pain when the belly is touched even lightly. **The person's life is in danger.** Take the person to a medical center **immediately** and on the way give ampicillin or penicillin (2 250-mg tablets or capsules every 6 hours) together with chloramphenicol or tetracycline (2 250-mg capsules every 6 hours), and very little water.

GENERAL FIRST AID

■ FEVER

Fever, or high body temperature, is not itself a sickness, but a symptom of many different illnesses.

TREATMENT:

☐ Uncover yourself completely. **Never** wrap yourself in clothing or blankets.

☐ Fresh air will not harm someone with fever. On the contrary, fresh air helps lower the fever.

☐ Take aspirin or acetaminophen (*Tylenol* or *Datril*) to lower fever.

☐ Drink lots of water, juices, or other liquids.

☐ When possible, find and treat the cause of the fever.

■ VERY HIGH FEVERS

A very high fever can be dangerous if it is not brought down quickly. It can cause convulsions or even permanent brain damage. High fever is most dangerous for small children.

TREATMENT:

☐ When a fever goes very high (over 104°F or 40°C), **it must be lowered at once:**

☐ Strip the person naked.

☐ Sponge the person's body with tepid (almost warm) water. (Cold water may work a little better, but can be painful to the victim, and can be dangerous since it may constrict the blood vessels of the skin.)

☐ Continue to sponge the victim until the fever goes down (below 101°F or 38°C).

- ☐ Give plenty of cool water to drink.

- ☐ Give medicine to bring down fever. Aspirin or acetaminophen (*Tylenol* or *Datril*) work well.

■ NOSEBLEEDS

TREATMENT:

- ☐ Sit quietly.

- ☐ Blow the nose to remove mucus and excess blood that has accumulated.

- ☐ Pinch the nose firmly for 10 minutes or until the bleeding has stopped.

- ☐ Breathe through the mouth.

- ☐ Lean forward with the head between the knees. Do not tilt the head back.

IF THIS DOES NOT CONTROL THE BLEEDING:

- ☐ Pack the nostril with a wad of cotton, leaving part of it outside the nose. If possible, first wet the cotton with hydrogen peroxide or *Vaseline.*

- ☐ Pinch the nose firmly again and don't let go for 10 minutes or more.

- ☐ Leave the cotton in place for a few hours after the bleeding stops; then take it out carefully.

Note: If your nose bleeds often, smear a little *Vaseline* inside the nostrils twice a day.

■ EYE INJURIES

Eye injuries must always receive immediate and careful attention. Even the most minor injury can result in total loss of vision if not cared for properly.

Note: If eye injury is caused by a caustic substance (acid, poison), **rinse with running water for more than 10 minutes** and seek medical attention quickly.

TREATMENT FOR OTHER EYE INJURIES:

- ☐ Gently wash away all dirt and debris with lukewarm boiled water.

- ☐ If there are blood clots attached to the eye, do not try to remove them.

- ☐ Care for eyelid injuries, if any (see below).

- ☐ Cover the eye with a bandage or patch and get medical help.

- ☐ If it will be more than 1 day before you can get medical help, give penicillin orally (1 250-mg tablet every 6 hours). Aspirin and codeine may be given every 4 hours to reduce pain.

- ☐ **Do not** try to remove foreign objects that are tightly stuck in the eyeball. Get medical help.

■ EYELID INJURIES

Eyelid injuries can be as serious as injuries to the eye itself, because if the eye is not continuously moistened by tears, which the lid spreads over it, it quickly dries, causing scarring or blindness.

TREATMENT:

- ☐ Wash away all dirt and foreign material with lukewarm boiled water.

- ☐ Return the torn or cut eyelid as closely as possible to its original position. Make sure the eye is completely covered.

- ☐ Bandage the eye snugly to hold the lid in place. Bandage the uninjured eye too, to prevent blinking or other eye movements that would disturb the position of the injured eyelid.

- ☐ Get medical help.

WOUNDS

■ CUTS, SCRAPES, AND SMALL WOUNDS

Cleanliness is of first importance in preventing infection and helping wounds to heal.

TREATMENT:

- ☐ First, wash your hands very well with soap and water.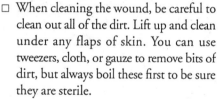

- ☐ Then wash the wound well with a nonirritating soap and cool, boiled water. If you do not have a mild soap, just use water.

- ☐ When cleaning the wound, be careful to clean out all of the dirt. Lift up and clean under any flaps of skin. You can use tweezers, cloth, or gauze to remove bits of dirt, but always boil these first to be sure they are sterile.

- ☐ Rinse the wound (for at least 5 minutes) with a saline solution of $3/4$ teaspoon of salt added to 1 quart (1 liter) of boiled water. **Be absolutely sure that no dirt or soap is left hidden in the cut.**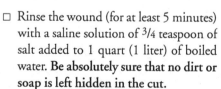

- ☐ After the wound has been cleaned, place a piece of light, clean gauze over the top. It should be light enough so that air can get to the wound and help it heal. Change the bandage every day and watch for signs of infection (see p. 157).

- ☐ If you are in an area where tetanus is common, you should get a tetanus booster (see p. 7).

- ☐ *Never* put alcohol, tincture of iodine, potassium permanganate, or *Merthiolate* directly into a wound; doing so will only damage the flesh and make healing slower.

■ LARGE CUTS

A recent cut that is very clean will heal faster if you bring the edges together so the cut stays closed. Close a deep cut only if all of the following are true:

☐ The cut is less than 12 hours old.

☐ The cut is very clean.

☐ It is impossible to get a health worker to close it the same day.

Before closing the cut, wash it very well with cool, boiled water and soap. Be absolutely sure that no dirt is left hidden in the cut.

There are two methods to close a cut, butterfly bandages of adhesive tape or sutures with thread.

Butterfly Bandages of Adhesive Tape

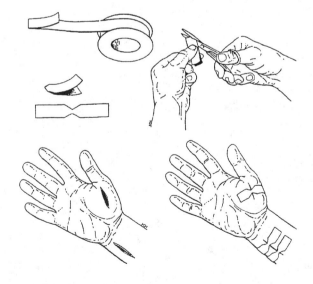

STITCHES OR SUTURES WITH THREAD

To find out if a cut needs stitches, see if the edges of the skin come together by themselves. If they do, usually no stitches are needed.

TO STITCH A WOUND:

☐ Boil a sewing needle and a thin thread (nylon or silk are best) for 10 minutes.

☐ Wash the wound with cool, boiled water and a nonirritating soap, as has been described.

☐ Wash your hands very well with boiled water and soap.

☐ Sew the wound like this:

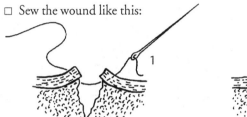 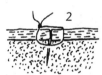

☐ Make the first stitch in the middle of the cut and tie it closed (figures 1 and 2).

☐ If the skin is tough, used boiled pliers to pull the needle through.

☐ Make enough other stitches to close the whole cut (figure 3).

Note: If the wound is deep (greater than $1/2$ inch or 1 cm), a stitch inside the wound as well as on the surface is necessary to prevent an abscess forming under the skin.

☐ Leave the stitches in place for 5-7 days (on the face 5 days; elsewhere, 7 days).

TO REMOVE THE STITCHES:

☐ Cut the thread on one side of the knot and pull the knot until the thread comes out.

Warning: Only close wounds that are very clean and less than 12 hours old. Old, dirty, or infected wounds must be left open. Bites from people, dogs, pigs, or other animals should also be left open. Closing them can cause dangerous infections.

If the wound that has been closed shows any signs of infection, remove the stitches immediately and leave the wound open.

■ BANDAGES

Bandages are used to keep wounds clean. For this reason, only use sterile (clean) bandages or pieces of cloth when covering wounds. If possible, cover the wound with a sterile gauze pad before bandaging. **It is better to have no bandage at all than one that is dirty or wet.**

EXAMPLES OF BANDAGES

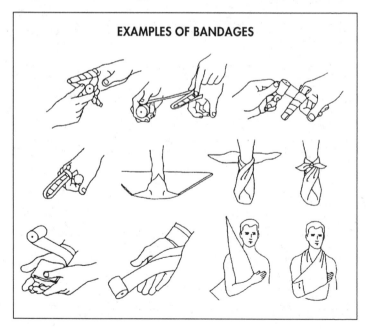

If a bandage gets wet or dirt gets under it, take the bandage off, wash the cut again, and put on a clean bandage.

Caution: Be careful that a bandage that goes around a limb is not so tight that it cuts off the flow of blood. If it feels too tight, or if your fingers or toes get cold, white, or blue, take the bandage off and wrap it again more loosely.

Many small scrapes and cuts do not need bandages. They heal best if washed with soap and cool, boiled water, rinsed well and left open to the air. The most important thing is to keep them clean.

■ INFECTED WOUNDS

A WOUND IS INFECTED IF:

☐ it becomes red, swollen, hot and painful,

☐ it has pus, or

☐ it begins to smell bad.

THE INFECTION IS SPREADING TO OTHER PARTS OF THE BODY IF:

☐ it causes fever,

☐ there is a red line above the wound, or

☐ the lymph nodes become swollen and tender.

TREATMENT OF INFECTED WOUNDS

☐ Put hot compresses over the wound for 20 minutes 4 times a day. Hold an infected hand or foot in a bucket of hot water with soap or potassium permanganate (1 teaspoon to a bucket).

☐ Keep the infected part at rest and elevated (raised above the level of the heart).

☐ If the infection is severe, use an antibiotic like penicillin or tetracycline, 1 250-mg tablet, 4 times a day.

Warning: If the wound has a bad smell, if brown or gray liquid oozes out, or if the skin around it turns black and forms air bubbles or blisters, this may be gangrene. **Seek medical help fast.**

Lymph nodes, often called "glands," are little traps for bacteria; they form small lumps under the skin when they get infected.

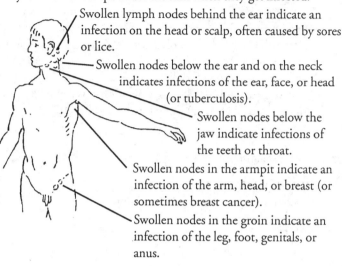

Swollen lymph nodes behind the ear indicate an infection on the head or scalp, often caused by sores or lice.

Swollen nodes below the ear and on the neck indicates infections of the ear, face, or head (or tuberculosis).

Swollen nodes below the jaw indicate infections of the teeth or throat.

Swollen nodes in the armpit indicate an infection of the arm, head, or breast (or sometimes breast cancer).

Swollen nodes in the groin indicate an infection of the leg, foot, genitals, or anus.

■ WOUNDS THAT ARE LIKELY TO BECOME DANGEROUSLY INFECTED:

☐ Dirty wounds, or wounds made by dirty objects.

☐ Puncture wounds and other deep wounds that do not bleed much.

☐ Wounds that occur where animals are kept: in corrals, pig pens, etc.

☐ Large wounds with severe crushing or bruising.

☐ Bites, especially from pigs, dogs, or people.

☐ Bullet wounds.

TREATMENT OF "HIGH RISK" WOUNDS:

☐ Like other wounds, wash well with cool, boiled water and soap. Remove all pieces of dirt, blood clots, and dead or badly damaged flesh. Squirt out the dirt using a syringe or suction bulb.

☐ Get medical attention.

☐ If the wound is very deep, if it is a bite, or if there is a chance that it still has dirt in it, the injured person should take an antibiotic, especially if the wound is on the hands or face. The best is erythromycin, in capsules (1 250-mg capsule, 4 times a day). In the most serious cases, injections of an antibiotic may be used.

☐ **Never** close this type of wound with stitches or "butterfly" bandages. **Leave the wound open.** If the wound is very large, a doctor may be able to close it later.

BURNS

∎ MINOR BURNS THAT DO NOT FORM BLISTERS (FIRST-DEGREE)

☐ To help ease the pain and lessen damage caused by a minor burn, put the burned part in cold (preferably, ice) water at once; leave the part immersed for 20 minutes. Take aspirin for pain.

☐ No other treatment is needed.

∎ BURNS THAT CAUSE BLISTERS (SECOND-DEGREE)

☐ Immerse in cold water as with first-degree burns.

☐ Apply dry, sterile gauze or cloth as a protective dressing.

☐ Get medical attention.

☐ Do not break blisters.

☐ If the blisters are broken, wash gently with boiled water that has been cooled. Cut off dead skin, then cover with thin, sterile gauze or cloth. Change every 24 hours.

☐ Keep the burned part elevated.

□ **It is very important to keep the burn as clean as possible. Protect it from dirt, dust, and flies.**

□ If signs of infection appear—pus, bad smell, fever, or swollen lymph nodes—apply compresses of warm salt water (1 teaspoon salt to 1 quart or 1 liter water) 3 times a day. Boil both the water and cloth before use. With great care, remove the dead skin and flesh.

■ DEEP BURNS (THIRD-DEGREE)

□ Deep burns that destroy the skin and expose raw or charred flesh are always serious, as are any burns that cover large areas of the body. Take the person to a health center at once. In the meantime, wrap the burned part with a very clean cloth or towel.

□ If there is a delay in getting medical help, treat the burn as described for second-degree burns. Leave the burn in the open air, covering it only with a loose cotton cloth or sheet to protect it from dust and flies. Keep the cloth very clean and change it each time it gets dirty with liquid or blood from the burn. Toxoid penicillin (2 250-mg tablets 4 times a day) and a tetanus booster (if not received in the last 5 years) may be given to prevent infection.

SPECIAL PRECAUTIONS FOR VERY SERIOUS BURNS

□ Any person who has been badly burned can easily go into **shock** (see pp. 144-145) because of combined pain, fear, and the loss of body fluids from the oozing burn.

□ Comfort and reassure the burned person. Give aspirin for pain and codeine if you can get it. Bathing open wounds in cool, slightly salty water also helps calm pain. Use 1 teaspoon salt for each quart (liter) of boiled (and cooled) water.

□ Give the burned person plenty of liquids (so long as the person is not vomiting and has no belly wound). If the burned area is large (more than twice the size of an adult hand), give the oral rehydration drink described on p. 50.

□ The burned person should drink the oral rehydration drink as often as possible until urination is frequent. Check to see if the urine is clear; if not, give the person more fluids.

□ It is important for persons who are badly burned to eat foods rich in protein. No type of food needs to be avoided.

■ BURNS AROUND THE JOINTS

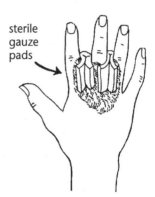

sterile gauze pads

When someone is badly burned between the fingers, in the armpit, or at other joints, gauze pads should be put between the burned surfaces to prevent them from growing together as they heal. Also, fingers, arms, and legs should be gently straightened and bent completely several times a day while healing. This is painful but helps prevent stiff scars that limit movement.

SPRAINS AND BROKEN OR DISLOCATED BONES

■ SPRAINS AND STRAINS

It is often difficult to know whether a hand or foot is bruised, sprained, or broken. It may be necessary to have an X ray taken.

TREATMENT:

□ Keep the joint motionless.

□ Wrap it with something that gives firm support.

□ For a twisted ankle, start at the foot and wind up to above the ankle joint.

□ Serious sprains take at least 3-4 weeks to heal. Broken bones take longer.

☐ You can keep the twisted joint in the correct position for healing by using an elastic bandage. Check often to make sure circulation has not been cut off. If the bandage feels too tight, or if the person's fingers or toes become cold, white, or blue, take the bandage off and wrap it again more loosely.

Caution: If the foot seems very loose or "floppy," or if the person has trouble moving the toes, get medical help. Surgery may be needed.

TO RELIEVE PAIN AND SWELLING:

☐ Keep the sprained part raised high.

☐ During the first 24 hours, put ice or cold, wet cloths over the swollen joint. Remove these for a few minutes every 20 minutes.

☐ Take aspirin.

☐ Stay off the sprain.

☐ After 48 hours, soak the sprain in warm water several times a day.

☐ Use a cane or crutches as the sprain recovers.

☐ Never rub or massage a sprain or broken bone. It does no good and can do more harm.

■ BROKEN BONES (FRACTURES)

A broken bone requires the attention of a doctor or trained health worker. A person with a broken bone should get medical attention as quickly as possible.

SYMPTOMS:

☐ Tenderness over the injury with pain on movement.

☐ Inability to move the injured part.

☐ Unnatural shape.

☐ Swelling and discoloration of the skin around the break.

TREATMENT:

☐ When a bone has been broken, the most important first step is to **keep the bone in a fixed position**. This prevents more damage (broken ends of bone can cut nerves, blood vessels, etc.).

☐ If there is a wound or bleeding, stop the bleeding first.

☐ Before trying to move or carry a person with a broken bone, keep the bone from moving with splints. Splints should extend from above the joint above the fracture to below the joint below the fracture.

☐ Pad splints well with soft material and tie them securely at several points (but not so tight as to interfere with circulation; check the pulse if not sure).

☐ One of the quickest ways to splint a broken leg is by tying it to the uninjured leg. Use wide bandages or strips of cloth; never use narrow rope or wire. Use padding between the legs, and tie them at several points above and below the break; tie the feet together.

☐ Support a broken arm or shoulder with a sling (but don't try to bend an injured elbow if it is straight).

BROKEN NECKS AND BACKS:

If there is any chance a person's back or neck has been broken, be very careful when moving the person. Try not to change the body's position. If possible, bring in a health worker before moving the injured person—otherwise, do so without bending the back or neck. For instructions on how to move an injured person, see pp. 156-157.

BROKEN RIBS:

These are very painful, but almost always heal on their own. It is better not to splint or bind the chest. The best treatment is to take aspirin—and rest. It may take months before the pain is gone completely.

A broken rib does not often puncture a lung, but if the person coughs blood or develops breathing difficulties, use antibiotics (penicillin or ampicillin) and seek medical help.

BROKEN THIGH BONE:

A broken upper leg, hip, or pelvis often needs special attention. It is best to splint the whole body like this:

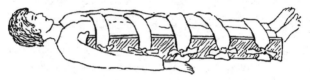

and to take the injured person to a health center at once.

■ COMPOUND FRACTURES

Compound fractures are broken bones that break through the skin. Since the danger of infection is very great in these cases, it is always better to get help from a health worker or doctor in caring for the injury.

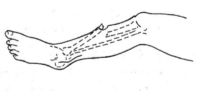

IF MEDICAL CARE IS NOT IMMEDIATELY AVAILABLE:

☐ Clean the wound and the exposed bone very thoroughly with boiled (and cooled) water and cover it lightly with a clean cloth.

☐ **Never put the bone back into the wound until the wound and the bone are absolutely clean.**

☐ Splint the wound to prevent more injury.

☐ If the bone has broken the skin, use an antibiotic immediately to prevent infections: penicillin or ampicillin, 2 250-mg capsules or tablets, 4 times a day.

Caution: Never rub or massage a broken limb or a limb that may possibly be broken.

■ DISLOCATIONS

Dislocations are bones that have come out of place at a joint. They are very painful and the person usually cannot move the injured part.

If medical help is nearby, have a doctor come to set the dislocation. In the meantime, splint the injured part as it is. Cold, wet cloths applied to the dislocated joint help lessen the pain.

If a doctor cannot come soon, try to put the bone back into place yourself. **The sooner the dislocation is set, the better.** Then keep it bandaged firmly in place so it does not slip out again (about a month). Avoid forceful use of the limb long enough for the joint to heal completely (2-3 months).

TO SET A DISLOCATED FINGER:

☐ Hold the hand firmly with one of your hands. With your other hand, slowly pull the end of the dislocated finger in a straight line with the hand until it slips into place.

TO SET A DISLOCATED JAW:

☐ (This is a very painful dislocation and should be set at once.) Protect your thumbs with several layers of bandage or cloth and put them into the person's mouth far back on the lower teeth. Your fingers should be under the chin. Press steadily down and back with the thumbs on the back teeth; pull up with the fingers under the chin.

TO SET A DISLOCATED SHOULDER:

☐ Lie down on the floor next to the injured person. Put your bare foot in the person's armpit and pull the arm slowly downward, at an angle to the body, as shown (1), using steady force for 10 minutes.

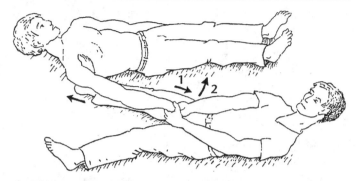

☐ Then, using your foot to position the bone, swing the arm closer to the person's body (2). The shoulder should "pop" back into place.

☐ After the shoulder is in place, bandage the arm firmly against the body. Keep it bandaged for a month. To prevent the shoulder from becoming completely stiff, adults should unbandage the arm for a few minutes, 3 times a day and, with the arm hanging at the side, move it gently in narrow circles.

☐ If there is an open wound near the joint, or if you cannot put the dislocated limb back in place, look for medical help at once. The longer you wait, the harder it will be to correct.

■ HOW TO MOVE A BADLY INJURED PERSON

☐ With great care, lift the injured person without bending the body anywhere.

☐ Have another person put the stretcher in place.

☐ Make sure that the head and neck do not bend.

☐ With the help of everyone, place the injured person carefully on the stretcher.

☐ If the neck is injured or broken, put bags of sand or tightly folded clothing on each side of the head to keep it from moving.

sand bags

BITES AND STINGS

■ SNAKES

Snakes are defensive animals and rarely attack unless provoked.

PREVENTION:

☐ Wear proper clothing and shoes. Do not wear shorts or sandals when traveling in areas where snakes are common.

☐ Do not bother or handle snakes.

☐ Do not put your hands into long grass, logs, or trees without inspecting these areas first.

☐ Use a flashlight at night.

☐ Know what types of snakes are in your area and what their habits are.

TREATMENT:

Every snakebite, whether poisonous or nonpoisonous, should receive medical attention. Aside from this, few experts agree on what first aid is best, particularly since different snakes and varying circumstances require different treatments. The following steps are generally agreed upon and should be carried out **immediately:**

☐ **Do not panic.** The victim should stay still and calm since movement circulates the poison through the body more quickly. Death from snakebite is rare.

☐ Use the *Sawyer Extractor* to remove the venom if you have it (see p. 17). Otherwise, it is best to begin immobilizing the part immediately.

☐ **Wrap the bitten area with a bandage.** You must apply pressure to the bitten area **immediately** by wrapping the limb with wide bandages or strips of cloth. The bandages should be as tight as you would use for a sprained ankle (i.e., do not cut off blood flow).

☐ **Splint the bitten arm or leg.** This is to keep the limb as still as possible. The splint and bandage should be left on until a medical facility is reached.

☐ **Identify the snake** or kill it if it can be done without risk or delay. Identification will aid the health worker or doctor in determining whether antitoxin should be given, and if so, what type. Do not directly handle the dead snake; carry it to the medical facility on a stick or in a bag.

☐ **Transport the victim to medical care.** Use a stretcher if available. The victim should not walk.

☐ **Give liquids.** The victim should drink as much as possible, but should *not* drink alcohol.

☐ **Give antivenin.** If the snake is poisonous, the doctor may inject antivenin. This should be done as soon as possible.

IMPORTANT!:

☐ *Do Not* cut over the fang marks and suck out the poison. Most experts feel that this method is ineffective and may cause unnecessary infection.

☐ *Do Not* use a tourniquet (a tight band or bandage that cuts off blood flow to the limb).

☐ *Do Not* use ice.

■ SEA SNAKES

All sea snakes are poisonous. They will not usually bite unless molested in the water or handled when they have been stranded on the beach. Sometimes their bite may only feel like a pinprick, and the reaction, although severe, may not set in until hours later. There is no antivenin for this type of poison, and the fatality rate is about 40%.

A bitten person should be evacuated immediately to a medical center that has facilities for artificial and assisted respiration.

■ POISONOUS SEA CREATURES

Varieties of the following sea creatures may be poisonous:
- ☐ Jellyfish.

- ☐ Portuguese man-of-war.

- ☐ Cone shells—sea mollusks with attractive, usually multicolored shells. **All the tropical varieties are poisonous.**

- ☐ Octopi—some small species are **very poisonous**.

- ☐ Stingrays.

- ☐ Lionfish, stonefish, scorpion fish. Very poisonous. Usually they are brightly colored and have long spines. Contact with the spines injects the venom, which causes agonizing pain and sometimes shock, heart irregularities, etc. If you plan to swim in tropical waters, find out what these fish look like and be alert.

- ☐ Fish and sharks with poison spines.

- ☐ Sea urchins.

PREVENTION: The best prevention for all the above animals is avoidance! Ask local people what to look out for in the water.

TREATMENT:
- ☐ Remove tentacles or spines.

☐ Wash area with rubbing alcohol or ammonia diluted with water (this will sting).

☐ Wrap area with cloth.

☐ Get medical help.

■ SCORPIONS

Some scorpions are far more poisonous than others. To adults, scorpion stings are rarely dangerous. Take aspirin and if possible put ice on the sting. For the numbness and pain that some-times last weeks or months, hot com-presses may be helpful.

■ LEECHES

When you see a leech on your skin (you usually can't feel them), use insect repellent, vinegar, lemon juice, salt, a cigarette, or a match to make them fall off—or they will fall off by themselves when satiated. Don't tear them off as bites can become inflamed.

■ TICKS

Ticks usually live in forested or grassy environments. Be sure to check your body if you have been in a tick-infested area. Although tick bites are not usually harmful, in some regions ticks can transmit serious diseases (see chapter 6).

TREATMENT:

☐ Do not simply try to pull the tick off. Pulling at a tick may leave the head and pinchers in your skin, resulting in infection or disease.

☐ Try to get the tick to "let go" by covering it with petroleum jelly (*Vaseline*), alcohol, oil, or gasoline. The tick should release its hold in a few minutes and you will be able to pull it out with tweezers.

☐ After a tick has been removed, wash the bite with soap and clean water.

☐ Watch for infection or signs of disease in the following days.

After You Return Home

■ GET A PHYSICAL CHECK-UP

Whether you were sick or not while in the Third World, you may have carried a disease or parasite home with you. It is a good idea to get a physical check-up when you return, especially if you were in remote areas for more than a couple of months. This physical should include a blood test, a tuberculin skin test, a stool examination for intestinal parasites, and, perhaps, a chest X ray.

■ MALARIA PILLS AFTER YOU RETURN HOME

As mentioned earlier, it is very important to continue taking malaria pills for 6 weeks after you return home (or after you leave the malarious area). This is necessary because most strains of malaria cycle between the bloodstream and the liver, yet the primary antimalarial drugs (chloroquine, mefloquine, *Fansidar,* and doxycycline) only prevent multiplication of the malaria parasites while the parasites are in the bloodstream. Continuing to take malaria pills for several weeks after possible exposure ensures that all of the parasites have cycled through the blood and been killed off.

Some types of malaria, however, have a residual form which persists in the liver and may not be eliminated during this 6-week period. These strains can lie dormant for long periods and cause relapses long after a traveler has returned home. If you were in a malarious area and develop a severe fever after you return, **see a doctor immediately** and report your possible exposure to malaria. Delayed attacks have been known to occur as long as 3 years after exposure to malaria.

If you were heavily exposed to mosquitoes in a malarious area, it may be appropriate for you to take **primaquine**, the "radical cure" for malaria, upon your return. Unlike the other drugs, primaquine kills the forms of malaria found in liver cells. **Warning:** Primaquine can cause severe side effects in people who are glucose-6-phosphate dehydrogenase (G6PD) deficient. (This enzyme problem is particularly common in blacks and persons of Asian or Mediterranean descent.) Before you use primaquine, you should be tested for G6PD deficiency at a medical laboratory.

Primaquine is taken daily for 14 days after leaving the malarious area, but before discontinuing the chloroquine. Primaquine should be taken *only* under a doctor's supervision.

Note: You can not donate blood for 3 years after you have been to a malarious area and taken antimalarial drugs.

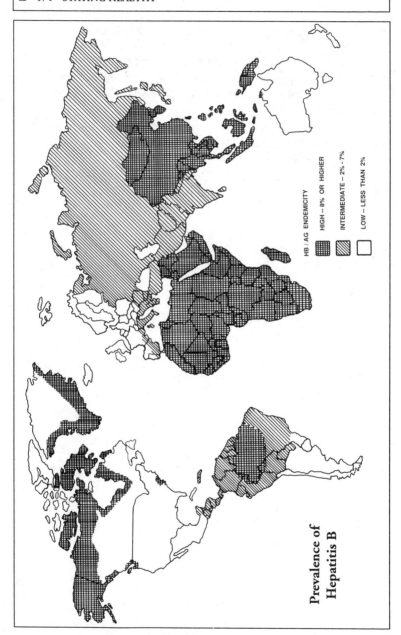

Prevalence of
Hepatitis B

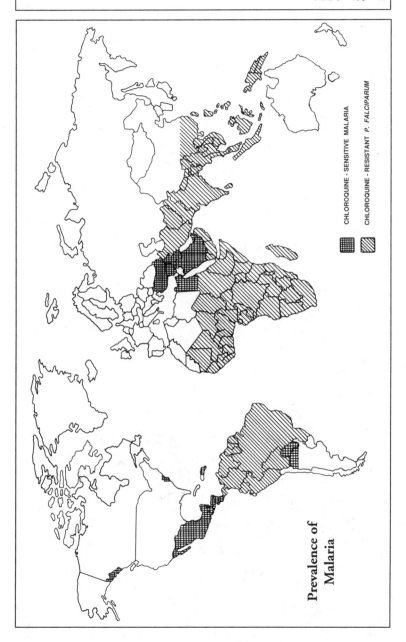

CHLOROQUINE - SENSITIVE MALARIA

CHLOROQUINE - RESISTANT *P. FALCIPARUM*

Prevalence of
Malaria

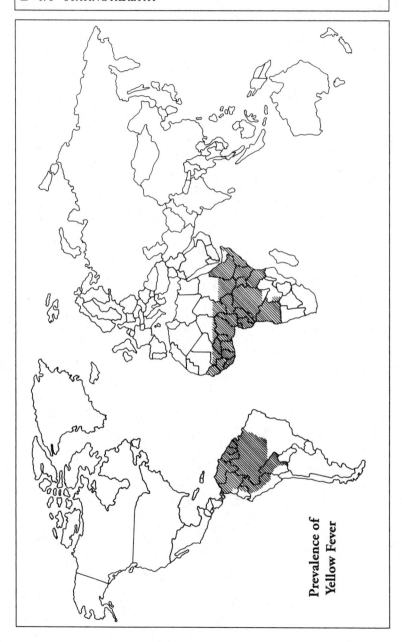

**Prevalence of
Yellow Fever**

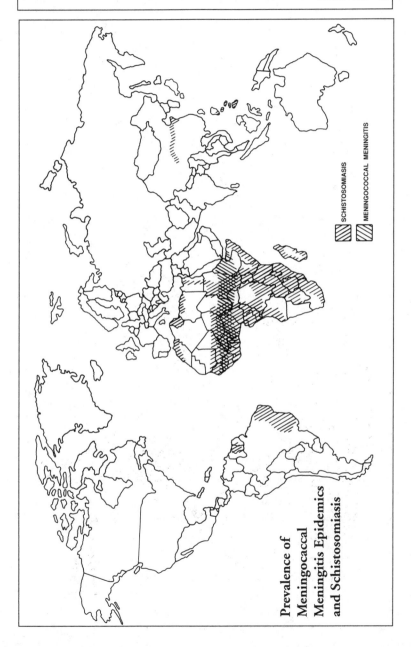

Prevalence of Meningocaccal Meningitis Epidemics and Schistosomiasis

SCHISTOSOMIASIS

MENINGOCOCCAL MENINGITIS

Booklist

A.M.C. Staff and Kathleen A. Homdal. *American Red Cross Safety and First Aid Handbook*. Denver: Little Books, 1992. $14.95.

Barnhart, R. *Physicians Desk Reference: PDR*. Oradell, NJ: Medical Economics Books, 1990. Comprehensive source for symptoms and treatment of diseases. Heavy use of medical terminology calls for a medical dictionary if you aren't a professional.

Douglas, Paul Harding, and Laura Pinsley. *The Essential AIDS Fact Book*. New York: Pocket Books, 1992. 128 pages, $6.00. Up-to-date, nontechnical guide to prevention of and testing for HIV as well as treatment.

Findlay, Russell E. *Snake Venom Poisoning*. Port Washington, NY: Scholium International, Inc., 1983. 576 pages, $57.50. The standard comprehensive text on poisonous snakes and snakebites throughout the world.

Hackett, Peter H. *Mountain Sickness: Prevention, Recognition, and Treatment*. 5th ed. New York: American Alpine Club, 1980. $6.00. Prevention and treatment of ailments suffered at high altitudes. Concise and well-written.

Hatt, John. *The Tropical Traveller*. New York: Hippocrene, 1984. 253 pages, $6.95. A readable book covering such topics as what to bring, theft, transportation, communication, and culture shock.

Lappe, Frances Moore. *Diet for a Small Planet*. 11th ed. New York: Ballantine Books, 1982. $5.95. Excellent explanation of complementary proteins, with examples and recipes.

The Boston Women's Health Book Collective. *The New Our Bodies, Ourselves*. New York: Simon & Schuster, 1985. 647 pages, $17.95. A book by and for women covering health maintenence, nutrition, self-defense, birth control, abortion, pregnancy, etc. A complete source-book; illustrated.

U.S. Department of Health and Human Services. *Health Information for International Travel* (The Yellow Book). Washington: USGPO, 1990. 174 pages, $5.00. The authoritative guide to vaccinations, malaria pills, and tropical diseases to which the traveler is at risk. Includes a country-by-country listing of vaccination requirements and recommendations, also a geographic distribution of health hazards. Somewhat technical.

Werner, David. *Where There is No Doctor.* 6th ed. Palo Alto: The Hesperian Foundation, 1992. 504 pages, $14.00. A complete village health care handbook. Includes information on children's health, pregnancy, use of drugs with dosages, thorough explanations of prevention and treatment of diseases, and first aid. Written in simple, nontechnical language; lots of illustrations. (Available from bookstores or The Hesperian Foundation, P.O. Box 1692, Palo Alto, California 94302; 415-325-9017.)

Wilkerson, James A. *Medicine for Mountaineering.* 3rd ed. Seattle: The Mountaineers Books, 1985. 376 pages, $12.95. Detailed first aid and general health information written for climbers in remote areas. Clearly written; illustrated.

Index

MOON HANDBOOKS—
THE IDEAL TRAVELING COMPANIONS

Open a Moon Handbook and you're opening your eyes and heart to the world. Thoughtful, sensitive, and provocative, Moon Handbooks encourage an intimate understanding of a region, from its culture and history to essential practicalities. Fun to read and packed with valuable information on accommodations, dining, recreation, plus indispensable travel tips, detailed maps, charts, illustrations, photos, glossaries, and indexes, Moon Handbooks are ideal traveling companions: informative, entertaining, and highly practical.

To locate the bookstore nearest you that carries Moon Travel Handbooks or to order directly from Moon Publications, call (800) 345-5473, Monday-Friday, 9 a.m.-5 p.m. PST.

THE PACIFIC/ASIA SERIES

BALI HANDBOOK   by Bill Dalton
Detailed travel information on the most famous island in the world. 428 pages.
$12.95

BANGKOK HANDBOOK   by Michael Buckley
Your tour guide through this exotic and dynamic city reveals the affordable and accessible possibilities. Thai phrasebook. 214 pages.   **$10.95**

BLUEPRINT FOR PARADISE: How to Live on a Tropic Island
by Ross Norgrove
This one-of-a-kind guide has everything you need to know about moving to and living comfortably on a tropical island. 212 pages.   **$14.95**

FIJI ISLANDS HANDBOOK   by David Stanley
The first and still the best source of information on travel around this 322-island archipelago. Fijian glossary. 198 pages.   **$11.95**

INDONESIA HANDBOOK   by Bill Dalton
This one-volume encyclopedia explores island by island the many facets of this sprawling, kaleidoscopic island nation. Extensive Indonesian vocabulary.
1,000 pages.   **$19.95**

MICRONESIA HANDBOOK:
Guide to the Caroline, Gilbert, Mariana, and Marshall Islands
by David Stanley
Micronesia Handbook guides you on a real Pacific adventure all your own.
345 pages.   **$11.95**

NEW ZEALAND HANDBOOK   by Jane King
Introduces you to the people, places, history, and culture of this extraordinary land. 571 pages.   **$18.95**

OUTBACK AUSTRALIA HANDBOOK   by Marael Johnson
Australia is an endlessly fascinating, vast land, and *Outback Australia Handbook*
explores the cities and towns, sheep stations, and wilderness areas of the
Northern Territory, Western Australia, and South Australia. Full of travel tips and
cultural information for adventuring, relaxing, or just getting away from it all. 355
pages.   **$15.95**

PHILIPPINES HANDBOOK   by Peter Harper and Evelyn Peplow
Crammed with detailed information, *Philippines Handbook* equips the escapist,
hedonist, or business traveler with thorough coverage of the Philippines's color-
ful history, landscapes, and culture. 587 pages.   **$12.95**

SOUTHEAST ASIA HANDBOOK   by Carl Parkes
Helps the enlightened traveler discover the real Southeast Asia. 873 pages.
$16.95

SOUTH KOREA HANDBOOK   by Robert Nilsen
Whether you're visiting on business or searching for adventure, *South Korea
Handbook* is an invaluable companion. Korean glossary with useful notes on
speaking and reading the language. 548 pages.   **$14.95**

SOUTH PACIFIC HANDBOOK   by David Stanley
The original comprehensive guide to the 16 territories in the South Pacific.
740 pages.   **$19.95**

TAHITI-POLYNESIA HANDBOOK   by David Stanley
All five French-Polynesian archipelagoes are covered in this comprehensive
guide by Oceania's best-known travel writer. 235 pages.   **$11.95**

THAILAND HANDBOOK   by Carl Parkes
Presents the richest source of information on travel in Thailand. 568 pages.
$16.95

THE HAWAIIAN SERIES

BIG ISLAND OF HAWAII HANDBOOK   by J.D. Bisignani
An entertaining yet informative text packed with insider tips on accommodations,
dining, sports and outdoor activities, natural attractions, and must-see sights.
347 pages.   **$11.95**

HAWAII HANDBOOK   by J.D. Bisignani
Winner of the 1989 Hawaii Visitors Bureau's Best Guide Award and the Grand
Award for Excellence in Travel Journalism, this guide takes you beyond the glitz
and high-priced hype and leads you to a genuine Hawaiian experience. Covers all
8 Hawaiian Islands. 879 pages.   **$15.95**

KAUAI HANDBOOK   by J.D. Bisignani
Kauai Handbook is the perfect antidote to the workaday world. Hawaiian and
pidgin glossaries. 236 pages.   **$9.95**

MAUI HANDBOOK   by J.D. Bisignani
"No fool-'round" advice on accommodations, eateries, and recreation, plus a comprehensive introduction to island ways, geography, and history. Hawaiian and pidgin glossaries. 350 pages.   **$11.95**

OAHU HANDBOOK   by J.D. Bisignani
A handy guide to Honolulu, renowned surfing beaches, and Oahu's countless other diversions. Hawaiian and pidgin glossaries. 354 pages.   **$11.95**

THE AMERICAS SERIES

ALASKA-YUKON HANDBOOK   by Deke Castleman and Don Pitcher
Get the inside story, with plenty of well-seasoned advice to help you cover more miles on less money. 384 pages.   **$13.95**

ARIZONA TRAVELER'S HANDBOOK   by Bill Weir
This meticulously researched guide contains everything necessary to make Arizona accessible and enjoyable. 505 pages.   **$14.95**

BAJA HANDBOOK   by Joe Cummings
A comprehensive guide with all the travel information and background on the land, history, and culture of this untamed thousand-mile-long peninsula. 356 pages.   **$13.95**

BELIZE HANDBOOK   by Chicki Mallan
Complete with detailed maps, practical information, and an overview of the area's flamboyant history, culture, and geographical features, *Belize Handbook* is the only comprehensive guide of its kind to this spectacular region. 212 pages.   **$13.95**

BRITISH COLUMBIA HANDBOOK   by Jane King
With an emphasis on outdoor adventures, this guide covers mainland British Columbia, Vancouver Island, the Queen Charlotte Islands, and the Canadian Rockies. 381 pages.   **$13.95**

CANCUN HANDBOOK   by Chicki Mallan
Covers the city's luxury scene as well as more modest attractions, plus many side trips to unspoiled beaches and Mayan ruins. Spanish glossary. 257 pages.   **$12.95**

CATALINA ISLAND HANDBOOK: A Guide to California's Channel Islands
by Chicki Mallan
A complete guide to these remarkable islands, from the windy solitude of the Channel Islands National Marine Sanctuary to bustling Avalon. 245 pages.   **$10.95**

COLORADO HANDBOOK   by Stephen Metzger
Essential details to the all-season possibilities in Colorado fill this guide. Practical travel tips combine with recreation—skiing, nightlife, and wilderness exploration—plus entertaining essays. 422 pages.   **$15.95**

IDAHO HANDBOOK   by Bill Loftus
A year-round guide to everything in this outdoor wonderland, from whitewater adventures to rural hideaways. 275 pages.   **$12.95**

JAMAICA HANDBOOK   by Karl Luntta
From the sun and surf of Montego Bay and Ocho Rios to the cool slopes of the Blue Mountains, author Karl Luntta offers island-seekers a perceptive, personal view of Jamaica. 213 pages.   **$12.95**

MONTANA HANDBOOK   by W.C. McRae and Judy Jewell
The wild West is yours with this extensive guide to the Treasure State, complete with travel practicalities, history, and lively essays on Montana life.
393 pages.   **$13.95**

NEVADA HANDBOOK   by Deke Castleman
Nevada Handbook puts the Silver State into perspective and makes it manageable and affordable. 400 pages.   **$14.95**

NEW MEXICO HANDBOOK   by Stephen Metzger
A close-up and complete look at every aspect of this wondrous state.
375 pages.   **$13.95**

NORTHERN CALIFORNIA HANDBOOK   by Kim Weir
An outstanding companion for imaginative travel in the territory north of the Tehachapis. 759 pages.   **$16.95**

OREGON HANDBOOK   by Stuart Warren and Ted Long Ishikawa
Brimming with travel practicalities and insider views on Oregon's history, culture, arts, and activities. 422 pages.   **$12.95**

TEXAS HANDBOOK   by Joe Cummings
Seasoned travel writer Joe Cummings brings an insider's perspective to his home state. 483 pages.   **$13.95**

UTAH HANDBOOK   by Bill Weir
Weir gives you all the carefully researched facts and background to make your visit a success. 445 pages.   **$14.95**

WASHINGTON HANDBOOK
by Dianne J. Boulerice Lyons and Archie Satterfield
Covers sights, shopping, services, transportation, and outdoor recreation, with complete listings for restaurants and accommodations. 433 pages.   **$13.95**

WYOMING HANDBOOK   by Don Pitcher
All you need to know to open the doors to this wide and wild state.
427 pages.   **$14.95**

YUCATAN HANDBOOK   by Chicki Mallan
All the information you'll need to guide you into every corner of this exotic land. Mayan and Spanish glossaries. 391 pages.   **$14.95**

THE INTERNATIONAL SERIES

EGYPT HANDBOOK   by Kathy Hansen
An invaluable resource for intelligent travel in Egypt. Arabic glossary.
510 pages.   **$18.95**

MOSCOW-ST. PETERSBURG HANDBOOK   by Masha Nordbye
Provides the visitor with an extensive introduction to the history, culture, and
people of these two great cities, as well as practical information on where to
stay, eat, and shop. 205 pages.   **$13.95**

NEPAL HANDBOOK   by Kerry Moran
Whether you're planning a week in Kathmandu or months out on the trail,
Nepal Handbook will take you into the heart of this Himalayan jewel.
378 pages.   **$12.95**

NEPALI AAMA   by Broughton Coburn
A delightful photo-journey into the life of a Gurung tribeswoman of Central
Nepal. Having lived with Aama (translated, "mother") for two years, first as an
outsider and later as an adopted member of the family, Coburn presents an
intimate glimpse into a culture alive with humor, folklore, religion, and ancient
rituals. 165 pages.   **$13.95**

PAKISTAN HANDBOOK   by Isobel Shaw
For armchair travelers and trekkers alike, the most detailed and authoritative
guide to Pakistan ever published. Urdu glossary. 478 pages.   **$15.95**

STAYING HEALTHY IN ASIA, AFRICA, AND LATIN AMERICA
by Dirk G. Schroeder, Sc D, MPH
Don't leave home without it! Besides providing a complete overview of the health
problems that exist in these areas, this book will help you determine which immunizations you'll need beforehand, what medications to take with you, and how
to recognize and treat infections and diseases. Includes extensively illustrated
first-aid information and precautions for heat, cold, and high altitude. 200 pages.
$10.95

**New travel handbooks may be available that are not on this list.
To find out more about current or upcoming titles,
call us toll-free at (800) 345-5473.**

IMPORTANT ORDERING INFORMATION

FOR FASTER SERVICE: Call to locate the bookstore nearest you that carries Moon Travel Handbooks or order directly from Moon Publications:

(800) 345-5473 • Monday-Friday • 9 a.m.-5 p.m. PST • fax (916) 345-6751

PRICES: All prices are subject to change. We always ship the most current edition. We will let you know if there is a price increase on the book you ordered.

SHIPPING & HANDLING OPTIONS: 1) Domestic UPS or USPS first class (allow 10 working days for delivery): $3.50 for the first item, 50 cents for each additional item.

Exceptions:
- **Moonbelt** shipping is $1.50 for one, 50 cents for each additional belt.
- Add $2.00 for same-day handling.
- UPS 2nd Day Air or Printed Airmail requires a special quote.
- International Surface Bookrate (8-12 weeks delivery): $3.00 for the first item, $1.00 for each additional item. Note: Moon Publications cannot guarantee international surface bookrate shipping.

FOREIGN ORDERS: All orders that originate outside the U.S.A. must be paid for with either an International Money Order or a check in U.S. currency drawn on a major U.S. bank based in the U.S.A.

TELEPHONE ORDERS: We accept Visa or MasterCard payments. Minimum order is US$15.00. Call in your order: (800) 345-5473, 9 a.m.-5 p.m. Pacific Standard Time.

ORDER FORM

Be sure to call (800) 345-5473 for current prices and editions or for the name of the bookstore nearest you that carries Moon Travel Handbooks • 9 a.m.–5 p.m. PST
(See important ordering information on preceding page)

Name: _____ Date: _____

Street: _____

City: _____ Daytime Phone: _____

State or Country: _____ Zip Code: _____

QUANTITY	TITLE	PRICE

Taxable Total_____

Sales Tax (7.25%) for California Residents_____

Shipping & Handling_____

TOTAL_____

Ship: ☐ UPS (no P.O. Boxes) ☐ 1st class ☐ International surface mail

Ship to: ☐ address above ☐ other _____

Make checks payable to: **MOON PUBLICATIONS, INC**. P.O. Box 3040, Chico, CA 95927-3040 U.S.A. We accept Visa and MasterCard. **To Order**: Call in your Visa or MasterCard number, or send a written order with your Visa or MasterCard number and expiration date clearly written.

Card Number: ☐ **Visa** ☐ **MasterCard**

☐ ☐ ☐ ☐ ☐ ☐ ☐ ☐ ☐ ☐ ☐ ☐ ☐ ☐ ☐ ☐

Exact Name on Card: _____

expiration date:_____

signature_____

SP/93

WHERE TO BUY THIS BOOK

BOOKSTORES AND LIBRARIES:
Moon Publications Handbooks are sold worldwide. Please write our sales manager for a list of wholesalers and distributors in your area that stock our travel handbooks.

TRAVELERS:
We would like to have Moon Publications Handbooks available throughout the world. Please ask your bookstore to write or call us for ordering information. If your bookstore will not order our guides for you, please write or call for a free catalog.

MOON PUBLICATIONS, INC.
P.O. BOX 3040
CHICO, CA 95927-3040 U.S.A.
TEL: (800) 345-5473
FAX: (916) 345-6751